The Basic Symbols
of the American
Political Tradition

Willmoore Kendall and
George W. Carey

The Basic Symbols of the American Political Tradition

with a new preface

The Catholic University of America Press
Washington, D.C.

The paper used in this publication meets the minimum requirements of
American National Standards for Information Science—Permanence of
Paper for Printed Library materials, ANSI Z39.48-1984.
∞

Library of Congress Cataloging-in-Publication Data
Kendall, Willmoore, 1909–1967.
    The basic symbols of the American political tradition / by Willmoore
Kendall and George W. Carey ; with a new preface.
        p.   cm.
    Originally published: Baton Rouge : Louisiana State University Press,
1970.
    Includes index.
    ISBN 0-8132-0826-2 (alk. paper)
    1. United States—Politics and government.   2. Political culture—
United States—History.   3. Political science—United States—History.
4. Elite (Social sciences)—United States—History.   5. Equality—United
States—History.   I. Carey, George Wescott, 1933–   .   II. Title.
JK39.K35   1995
320.973—dc20   94-39960
                                                                      CIP

To my friend Willmoore
Requiescat in pace

Contents

Preface to This Edition

The Basic Symbols of the American Political Tradition (or just *Basic Symbols* as it has come to be known) first appeared more than twenty-five years ago. At that time it attracted some notoriety because neither its approach nor its interpretations readily fit into any of the major schools of thought dealing with the American political tradition. More significantly, it frontally challenged core tenets of what had become received wisdom concerning the roots of our political beliefs and institutions. Its central thesis concerning the nature and direction of our political tradition also aroused controversy. Briefly stated, this thesis holds that we have moved away from the unique and defining principles and practices central to the political tradition of our Founding Fathers, those associated with self-government by a virtuous people deliberating under God. In their place, it is contended, we have embraced a new, largely contrived, "tradition" derived from the language of the Declaration of Independence with "equality" and "rights" at its center.

The publication of this new paperback edition presents an excellent opportunity to elaborate on this thesis by detailing more fully the bases for maintaining that our political tradition has been "derailed" in the sense indicated above, and by answering, if only by indirection in some cases, those who have taken exception with one or more of its constituent elements. The reasons why *Basic Symbols* stands well outside the prevailing schools of thought regarding our political tradition, and why it will likely remain so for the indefinite future, should be apparent from this undertaking.

We can perhaps best approach the underlying foundations of the derailment thesis by focusing on one aspect of our tradition, as pictured by Progressive historians, that is now widely accepted as conventional wisdom. According to these historians, there is a major discontinuity or rupture in our political tradition. The political landscape, including fundamental political principles, outlook, and attitudes, they argue, changed dramatically between 1776 and 1787, during the interval between the Declaration of Independence and the drafting of the Constitution. Moreover, on their showing, one side of this great divide (the Declaration side) is marked by an altruism, a spirit of fraternity and democracy, and a love of liberty; the other (the Constitution side), by a concern for special interests, a distrust of the masses, and a fear of liberty.

This view of the tradition, particularly its constitutional side, seems to have originated in the early years of the twentieth century with the publication of James Allen Smith's *The Spirit of American Government*.[1] The third chapter of Smith's work assails the Framers and the Constitution. "The evidence is overwhelming," wrote Smith, "that the men who sat in that [the Constitutional] convention had no faith in the wisdom or political capacity of the people." "Their aim and purpose," he continued, "was not to secure a larger measure of democracy,

---

[1] *The Spirit of American Government* (New York: The Macmillan Company, 1907). This work was reprinted by Harvard University Press in 1965 with an insightful introduction by Cushing Strout. The citations below are to the Harvard edition.

Strout points out, "The original prophet of this new political vision," one that questioned the motives and wisdom of the Founding Fathers, "was James Allen Smith." "His theory about the aristocratic spirit of American government escaped the direct fire of historical criticism until the mid-1950s, if only because he himself was forgotten, and his ideas survived as a commonplace, a piece of mental furniture placed in a corner and neglected while the rest of the furnishings were done over in a new style" (xiv–xv). Among those who "reupholstered" Smith's basic thesis, according to Strout, were Richard Hofstadter (*The American Political Tradition*) and Merrill Jensen (*The New Nation*). On this matter see our discussion below.

but to eliminate as far as possible the direct influence of the people on legislation and public policy."[2] Smith's views were soon bolstered in certain important particulars by Charles A. Beard in his highly controversial *An Economic Interpretation of the Constitution of the United States.* Beard went beyond surveying the economic interests and motives of the Founding Fathers to stress the lack of popular participation in the processes leading up to the Philadelphia Convention, as well as in the struggle over ratification.[3] He went so far as to raise doubts whether even a majority of those who voted for delegates to the ratifying conventions in five states—among them New York and Virginia—supported ratification. Taken together, the works of Smith and Beard pictured the Constitution as a thoroughly undemocratic document, designed by elites bent on protecting the interests of vested minorities.

In stark contrast to this view of the Constitution, Smith portrayed the Declaration of Independence as the embodiment of democratic yearnings. He insisted that the Constitution was a "reactionary" document designed to stifle the "democratic tendencies" of the Declaration. He lamented that "the democratic tendency which manifested itself with the outbreak of the Revolution" gave way "a few years later to the political reaction which found expression in our present Constitution."[4] Smith's view, suffice it to say, is still a staple among historians and political scientists who study our founding era. For instance, Gordon Wood in his widely heralded *The Creation of the American Republic,* published more than sixty years after Smith's work, largely echoes this thesis: the Constitution, he writes, is no more than an "artificial contrivance" designed "to restore and to prolong the traditional kind of elitist influence in politics" that was being undermined by "social developments" spurred by the revolution. Like Smith, he concludes that the Constitu-

---

[2] Smith, *Spirit,* 32.
[3] Charles A. Beard, *An Economic Interpretation of the Constitution of the United States* (New York: The Macmillan Company, 1913), 324.
[4] Smith, *Spirit,* 28.

tion "was intrinsically an aristocratic document designed to check the democratic tendencies of the period."[5]

There are stimulating variations on this theme that also present us with greater insight into the opposing values and aspirations presumably marking this break in our tradition. Vernon Parrington in his two volume work, *Main Currents in American Thought*, pictured the founding era in terms of a clash between two basically antagonistic ideologies, "French romantic philosophy" and "English liberalism."[6] The basic tenets of this French romantic philosophy, according to Parrington, included the belief that "reason and not interests should determine social institutions; that the ultimate ends to be sought were universal liberty, equality, and fraternity";[7] that individuals should sublimate their self-interest for the common good; and that "as free men and equals it is the right and duty of citizens to recreate social and political institutions to the end that they shall further social justice, encouraging the good in men rather than perverting them to evil."[8] Moreover, this school of thought rejected the Puritan view of human nature as depraved and vicious, regarding it rather "as potentially excellent and capable of indefinite development." On the other hand, contended Parrington, English liberalism was "hostile to all the major premises and ideals of the French school." Marked by a realism and materialism, it regarded human nature as "acquisitive." Thus, its concerns were not those of social justice, the "rights of man," or the cooperative society, but instead with "the needs of a capitalist order."[9]

Parrington left little doubt which of these theories comes

---

[5] Gordon Wood, *The Creation of the American Republic* (Chapel Hill: University of North Carolina Press, 1969), 513.

[6] Vernon Parrington, *Main Currents in American Thought*, 2 vols. (New York: Harcourt, Brace and World, 1927).

[7] Parrington, vol. I, *The Colonial Mind (1620–1800)*, 275–76.

[8] Ibid., xi.

[9] Ibid.

closest to finding expression in the Constitution. The Founding Fathers, he wrote, wanted to protect private property from
the ravages of majorities. As "realists" they "followed the teachings of the greatest political thinkers from Aristotle to Locke
in asserting that the problem of government lay in arranging a
stable balance between the economic interests of the major
classes." They were, he added, oblivious to the "revolutionary
conception of equalitarianism, that asserted the rights of man
apart from property and superior to property."[10] Following
Beard, he argued that the shrewd political tactics and "skillful
propaganda" of the Federalists secured ratification of the Constitution in spite of majority opposition.[11]

The scope of Parrington's analysis embraces many strands of
thought that have emerged concerning the nature of the gulf
that presumably separates the Declaration from the Constitution. The Rousseauianism of the French romantic philosophy,
for instance, calls for the sublimation of private or particular
interests for the common good. As such it bears a very close
relationship to the concept of "civic humanism" central to
those who look at the founding period from the perspective of
classical republicanism.[12] Likewise, Parrington's account of the
ideals associated with the French romantic school of thought,
particularly the yearnings for a cooperative society free from
the competition inherent in capitalism, parallels Herbert
Croly's earlier efforts to define the Progressive vision of the
promise of American life that we will survey below.

These variations, however, should not obscure the basic

---

[10] Ibid., 286.
[11] Ibid., 279.
[12] See, for example, J. G. A. Pocock, *The Machiavellian Moment* (Princeton:
Princeton University Press, 1975). According to Pocock, the key elements and concerns of "classical republicanism" as refined and perpetuated by Machiavelli, Bol-
ingbroke, Sydney, Harrington, and others found its way to America in the eighteenth century. According to Pocock, it has never entirely disappeared from
American thought, though by the time of the Constitution it no longer predomi-
nated.

theme of Progressive thought that has remained constant over
the decades: the Declaration is on the "angelic" side of a great
divide that separates it from the Constitution. The Declaration, as one careful student of the era has noted, is invariably
"portrayed as the ultimate expression of Revolutionary ideals,
to wit, egalitarianism, popular majority rule, and human
rights"; whereas the "Constitution is cast in the role of counter-
revolutionary reaction in support of monied privilege, minority rule, and property rights."[13] This view of the Constitution,
considered almost heretical when it was first advanced by
Smith and Beard, is now widely propagated in American history and government textbooks that deal with this era.[14] Aside
from being an obvious contributing factor to the derailment of
the earlier tradition, the widespread acceptance of this radically altered perspective of our founding also reflects the
extent of the derailment.

Now, as *Basic Symbols* points out, albeit in passing, the path
had been cleared much earlier for this Progressive treatment
of our tradition by Abraham Lincoln in his Gettysburg address.

[13] Robert F. Gibbs, "The Spirit of '89: Conservatism and Bicentenary," *The University Bookman* 14 (Spring 1974), 54.

[14] Douglass Adair, in a survey of American history texts in 1950, revealed a
"powerful influence still exerted by Beard's monograph" concerning the character and motives of the Framers. See "The Tenth Federalist Revisited," in *Fame and
the Founding Fathers*, ed. Trevor Colbourn (New York: W. W. Norton and Company,
1974), 76. Martin Diamond writing in 1974 remarks that "by the 1930's, in the
worlds of both social science and literary criticism, Smith, Beard, and Parrington
had achieved an amazing hegemony. Few who grew up in those years will have forgotten the sense of enlightenment, of emancipation, and of avant-garde intellectu-
alism that came as one discovered these authors or their views." By the 1970s these
same views, to quote Diamond, "darken the mood of the Bicentennial" and create
a "sense of faltering and uncertainty" about the relationship between the Declaration and the Constitution. "The Declaration and the Constitution: Liberty, Democracy, and the Founders," *Public Interest* 41 (Fall 1975), 45.

Diamond's position, like that of all other "Straussians" (i.e., students of the late
Professor Leo Strauss or those who have come to accept his principal teachings), is
that there is a continuity between the Declaration and the Constitution. They also
accept Lincoln's view of that relationship. See text below.

What Lincoln accomplished at Gettysburg is truly monumen-
tal. He turned our tradition upside down by linking our beginnings or "founding" as a united people with the Declaration of
Independence and by deriving a binding national commitment to the advancement of equality from its "all men are created equal" clause. As Garry Wills puts this, Lincoln "performed one of the most daring acts of open-air sleight-of-hand
ever witnessed by the unsuspecting.... The crowd departed
with a new thing in its ideological luggage, that new constitution Lincoln had substituted for the one they brought there
with them."[15] Indeed, as Wills maintains, the Gettysburg
address "has become an authoritative expression of American
spirit," maybe "even more influential" than the Declaration
"since it determines how we read the Declaration." In any
event, as Wills concludes, "Because of it [the Gettysburg
address], we live in a different America."[16]

The contention that Lincoln fostered the derailment of the
tradition is perhaps the most controversial single element in
the thesis advanced in *Basic Symbols*.[17] The most forceful rejoinder to this contention embraces two fundamental propositions
that can fairly be put as follows: first, Lincoln's account of our
political tradition and his conviction that the Declaration, as
our founding document, contains binding national commitments is "correct"; and second, Lincoln's views on the meaning of equality set forth in the Declaration of Independence
are not to be confused with those advanced by Progressivism
or welfare statism, much less the radical egalitarianism that has
emerged in recent decades.

While chapter five can be read as a specific answer to the
first proposition, most of *Basic Symbols* relates in one way or

---

[15] Garry Wills, *Lincoln at Gettysburg: The Words That Remade America* (New York:
Simon and Schuster, 1992), 38.

[16] Ibid., 146–47.

[17] This contention is critiqued extensively by Harry Jaffa in chapter 2, *How to
Think about the American Revolution* (Durham: Carolina Academic Press, 1978).

another to the status of the Declaration and the Constitution in the context of a political tradition that, in our view, stretches back to the first settlements on these shores. From our perspective, in other words, the founding era and its key documents must be viewed and understood in terms of a prior, indigenous, and coherent political tradition. When viewed from this perspective, as we endeavor to show, their character and relationship to one another are substantially different from that conveyed by Lincoln and the Progressives. This is a major theme of *Basic Symbols*, one that sets it apart from most other works in this area,[18] particularly those that mark the beginning of our political tradition with the Declaration of Independence. On this proposition, then, there is a definite parting of the ways between *Basic Symbols* and its critics, with little left to be said.

The second part of the rejoinder, however, raises an interesting question that is a matter of ongoing debate; namely, what is the relationship, if any, between Lincoln's position and that of the later Progressives, egalitarians, "reformers" and the like? In what sense, if any, can we say that Lincoln was the father of the modern, centralized, ever expanding, social welfare state that promotes egalitarianism? Lincoln's conservative defenders insist that Lincoln subscribed to a narrow view of equality; that his reference to equality in the Gettysburg address must be understood largely in light of the slavery issue.[19] And there is support for this position. In his reaction to the Dred Scott decision, for example, he reveals a less than expansive conception of what the authors of the Declaration meant by the "all

---

[18] A notable exception would be Donald S. Lutz, *The Origins of American Constitutionalism* (Baton Rouge: Louisiana State University Press, 1988).

[19] For a fine effort along these lines, particularly to "unlink" Lincoln from the Progressives, see Steven Hayward, "Whose Lincoln?" *Reason* 23 (May 1991). Hayward may be right in arguing that Lincoln's language and concerns place him well outside the Progressive camp. In our view, the linkage between Lincoln and modern egalitarians, even the most extreme, stems from the expansiveness and adaptiveness of Lincoln's conception of equality. See text below.

men are created equal" clause. He declares that while they did intend "to include *all* men, they did not intend to declare men equal *in all respects*" such as "color, size, intellectual, moral developments, or social capacity." "They defined with tolerable distinctness," he believed, "in what respects they did consider all men created equal—equal in 'certain inalienable rights, among which are life, liberty, and the pursuit of happiness.'" As if to answer those who contended that the authors of the Declaration did not regard slaves as equals, he maintains that they did not mean to assert "that all were then actually enjoying that equality, nor yet, that they were about to confer it immediately upon them"; something which, he observes "they had no power" to do. Rather, in his view, the authors "meant simply to declare the *right*, so that *enforcement* of it might follow as fast as circumstances should permit."[20]

The sentences that follow immediately upon these, however, convey a spirit and perspective that leave the door open to a more expansive view of equality, one that moves well beyond simply the slavery question. The authors of the Declaration, Lincoln contends, "meant to set up a standard maxim for free society, which should be familiar to all and revered by all; constantly looked to, constantly approximated, and thereby constantly spreading and deepening its influence, and augmenting the happiness and value of life to all people of all colors everywhere." Beyond this, he continues, the equality clause was really of no "practical use in effecting our separation from Great Britain"; it was, rather, intended "for future use" as, we must assume, the circumstances might warrant.[21] This observation is of some significance as well, for, by declaring the equal-

---

[20] Speech at Springfield, Illinois, June 26, 1857. *The Collected Works of Abraham Lincoln*, ed. Roy P. Basler, 9 vols. (New Brunswick: Rutgers University Press, 1953), Vol. 2, 405–6. Lincoln sees fit to quote and amplify upon this passage in his Alton debate (October 15, 1858) with Douglas. However, here he confines his remarks to the slavery issue. *The Lincoln-Douglas Debates*, ed. Harold Holzer (New York: Harper Collins, 1993), 343–44.

[21] Basler, ed., *Collected Works*, Vol. 2, 406.

ity clause independent of and even superfluous to the principal purpose of the Declaration, he has entirely removed from
consideration another and thoroughly legitimate interpretation of its meaning that does not embrace equality as a goal or
norm in the sense he means.[22] (On this point see Appendix I.)
Taken as a whole, these passages would suggest that he did
regard equality as a permanent and transcendent goal for all
"free" societies.[23]

Closely related to these remarks are other views he
expressed in considering the meaning and purpose of the
Civil War. After chastising the seceding states for leaving out of
their "Declarations of Independence" the "all men are created
equal" clause, as well as references to the "rights of men, and
the authority of the people," he goes on to write: "This is
essentially a People's contest. On the side of the Union, it is a
struggle for maintaining in the world, that form, and substance of government, whose leading object is, to elevate the
condition of men—to lift artificial weights from all shoul-
ders—to clear the paths of laudable pursuit for all—to afford
all, an unfettered start, and a fair chance, in the race of life.
Yielding to partial, and temporary departures, from necessity,
this is the leading object of the government for whose existence we contend."[24] Obviously, one could easily work from

[22] J. R. Pole argues that Lincoln adopted a universalist view of equality in the
Declaration, a rather "sweeping" conception of equality, rather than the narrow,
tenable, view that the "all men are created equal" clause meant only that "one people was the equal of another." *The Pursuit of Equality in American History* (Berkeley:
University of California Press, 1978), 55. On this point see text below.

[23] In this vein, Mortimer Adler writes that Lincoln's reference to "its future use"
serves to turn "our attention to the political significance of the truth concerning
human equality. Human equality—the personal equality of men as men, or of
human beings as human—is by no means the only equality with which we are concerned in our social lives. We are concerned with what, in contradistinction to *personal* equality, might be called *circumstantial* equality—that is, equality of conditions or results, equality of opportunity, and equality of treatment." *We Hold These
Truths: Understanding the Ideas and Ideals of the Constitution* (New York: Macmillan
Publishing Co., 1987), 45. Later Adler describes Lincoln's reference to "its future
use" as a "prophetic vision" (141).

[24] "Message to Congress in Special Session, July 4, 1861," *Collected Works*, IV, 438.

the language of "an unfettered start, and a fair chance" to derive mandates for government to pursue radical egalitarian policies far beyond those presently in place.

Bearing this in mind, it certainly is not unreasonable to associate Lincoln's words and thoughts with the egalitarianism that characterizes the modern, centralized, welfare state. It is entirely understandable why one contemporary student of the progress of equality in the United States can write: "Given the persistence of racial, sexual, and economic inequality, Lincoln's words have not lost their significance."[25] Nor is it difficult to see why others see the Gettysburg address, in particular, as not only articulating the purpose and meaning of the Civil War, but also setting the nation on the course of "constantly trying to enlarge the definition and deepen the meaning of 'all men are created equal.' "[26] Likewise, it is hard to fault Robert Bellah for seeing Lincoln, the Declaration of Independence, and the Gettysburg address as providing the nation with its "normative core," the "abstract propositions to which we [as a unified people] are dedicated." We can readily apprehend his argument that at the core of our "special civil religion" is the "all men are created" clause that points to a problem "more general" than slavery, namely, "how to actualize on this earth the great religious and moral insights that have been given to us."[27] Moreover, we can see why Mortimer J. Adler has come to regard the Declaration, the Constitution, and the Gettysburg address as embodying "the American testament," with the Declaration seen as providing us with "the nation's basic articles of political faith."[28] In sum, to go no further, Lincoln's works can be, and more frequently than not are, linked to a

[25] Charles Redenius, *The American Ideal of Equality* (Port Washington, N.Y.: Kennikat Press, 1981), 58.
[26] From the commentary of Ken Burns in the final episode of the Civil War documentary televised by PBS, quoted by Steven Hayward, "Whose Lincoln?" 26.
[27] "The Revolution and the Civil Religion," in *Religion and the American Revolution,* ed. Jerald C. Brauer, Sidney E. Mead, and Robert N. Bellah (Philadelphia: Fortress Press, 1976), 65.
[28] Adler, *We Hold These Truths,* 7.

broad conception of equality that is considered to be central to our political tradition.

Finally, to return briefly to Progressivism, we are hardly surprised that Herbert Croly, its leading theoretician, could write of Lincoln that "the life of no other American has revealed with anything like the same completeness the peculiar moral promise of genuine democracy."[29] While he is commonly called the "father" of the New Deal, Croly's concept of "genuine democracy" went well beyond regulation of the economy, aid for the needy, and a redistribution of wealth. His vision, as we have already remarked, closely resembles Parrington's French romanticism, in both its scope and its substance. It called for the "emancipation" of individuals that could only come about by diminishing "undesirable competition" and encouraging "desirable competition" through minimizing the "mercenary motive" and placing a premium on "excellence of work."[30] He sought to cultivate an environment in which individuals would make decisions, not in terms of their self-interest, but in light of the common good. "Not until" an individual's "action is dictated by disinterested motives," he wrote, "can there be ... harmony between private and public interests," a harmony that he believed essential for a "complete democracy." This state of affairs, he continued, could be satisfactorily achieved only "by the systematic authoritative transformation of the private interest of the individual into a disinterested devotion to a special project."[31] We need not concern ourselves with other facets of Croly's rather ambitious program, however, to see that he, too, must have apprehended Lincoln's vision of democracy to be animated by an egalitarian spirit.

[29] Herbert Croly, *The Promise of American Life* (New York: The Macmillan Company, 1909), 89.
[30] Ibid., 415.
[31] Ibid., 418.

Having noted this much, we must hasten to point out that the argument over the degree to which Lincoln's substantive notions of equality—that is, the specific content of his equality—give rise to or square with modern egalitarian beliefs and policies is not central to the thesis advanced in *Basic Symbols.* Rather, it is other attributes of his notion of equality—namely, that it is both universal and a seemingly transcendent goal whose realization is constantly to be striven for—that render it so inviting for modern egalitarians to use as a justification of, or source for, the advancement of their policies. Lincoln, for instance, could not say that his equality called only for the emancipation of slaves when circumstances permitted. On the contrary, its full realization clearly required the elimination of lesser inequalities of various kinds that stood in the way of the emancipated slaves obtaining full equality, as well as those unforseen inequalities that might arise over the course of time. Clearly his vision also called for the eradication of all such lesser inequalities that would prevent any group or individual, not just emancipated slaves, from realizing full equality within society. Thus, the concern over substance—that is, whether Lincoln would agree or not with this or that policy designed to fulfill our presumed commitment to equality—is really secondary to the fact that the character of his equality, particularly its open-endedness and universality, is so congenial to modern egalitarians.

Basic Symbols was written not to tarnish Lincoln's image, to defend the position of the slave-holding South, or to explore the ways, short of civil war, by which slavery might have been extinguished, but rather to identify the basic symbols of our political tradition, to outline the nature of their critical clarification over time, and, *inter alia,* to explain how it has come to pass that they have been replaced by new symbols through the derailment we have described above. It is true that *Basic Sym-*

bols does reflect a deep concern about the extent of the derailment and its consequences for the future of our nation. We admit that there is no way to measure precisely the degree to which the new tradition has taken hold. But to gain some appreciation and insight into the extent of our derailment, we can perhaps do no better than to consider only one aspect of Publius's argument against a bill of rights. When he wrote in Federalist 84 that "WE THE PEOPLE" is a "better recognition of popular rights" than those elaborated at length in the various state constitutions, and when he went on to contend that the Constitution itself was in every meaningful sense "A BILL OF RIGHTS," he was, in effect, asserting the primacy of deliberative self-government under the forms of the Constitution, a position thoroughly in keeping with the basic symbols of the tradition up to that time. Yet few today, it would seem, comprehend the tradition that formed the backdrop for his position. Even fewer would publicly support his position, so strong is the new tradition with its commitment to "rights."

Basic Symbols, if nothing else, raises important normative questions that relate to this derailment. Not the least of these concerns the changed character of our political regime. Our Constitution, consistent with the basic symbols, is clearly *nomocratic* in character, largely concerned, that is, with providing rules and limits for the government through which the people express their will. Since the derailment, however, the Constitution is increasingly viewed from a *teleocratic* perspective, as an instrument designed to fulfill the ends, commitments, or promises of the Declaration.[32] As this change takes hold, we

---

[32] We have borrowed the *nomocratic/teleocratic* framework from Michael Oakeshott. See his *On Human Conduct* (Oxford: Clarendon Press, 1975). For an interesting discussion of our founding and subsequent political developments that utilizes this framework see, M. E. Bradford, *Original Intentions: On the Making and Ratification of the United States Constitution* (Athens: University of Georgia Press, 1993).

This distinction can be drawn in other terms in the context of the American tradition, that is, between the "means" and the "ends" conceptions of republican-

witness an erosion of the constitutional processes and provisions designed to preserve and promote deliberative self-government. The legitimacy of policies and programs comes to depend on the ends they serve or advance, not on the means or processes by which they were adopted or promulgated. This trend, already evident when *Basic Symbols* first appeared, has grown more pronounced. The Supreme Court, for instance, has grown bolder and bolder in its usurpation of legislative powers, as we can readily see in its decisions on abortion, busing, affirmative action, prayer, and pornography, to name only a few. It has even assumed the power of the purse, long regarded as the exclusive prerogative of the legislature. But the new tradition serves, more convincingly now than at any other time in our history, to legitimize these and like developments—so long, that is, as the courts, the bureaucracy, or the president advance the ideals and goals of the new tradition.

This loss of self-government is no small matter. But even worse, as our final chapter indicates, is the fate that awaits us if we cannot find our way back to the basic symbols that guided our Founders. The critical question is whether the tradition of deliberative self-government can be restored before we suffer the full consequences of the derailment. If the developments of the last few decades are any indication, the prospects do not seem bright. But of this we may be sure: the task of restoration will not be easy.

---

ism. The ends school views republicanism as a way of life in which certain ideals are approximated or realized, whereas the means school looks upon republicanism primarily in terms of self-government and its decision-making institutions.

Preface to the Original Edition

Willmoore Kendall was invited to give a series of lectures at Vanderbilt University in the summer of 1964 on the American political tradition. These lectures, five in all, have been dubbed by Willmoore's colleagues and students "The Vanderbilt Lectures."

Soon after Willmoore's death, his wife asked me to assume the task of editing and expanding the lectures so that they would be suitable for a book. I readily agreed to this undertaking for reasons that are too numerous and complicated to cite here.

The following facts ought to be stated for the benefit of those who read this book:

(a) The first four chapters of this volume constitute the heart of the Vanderbilt lectures as they were delivered. These lectures, because they were designed for oral presentation required some editing and the adding of footnotes in order that they would be suitable for book form. I have tried to make only those revisions and additions necessary for that purpose.

(b) The last four chapters (with exceptions I will note immediately below) are mine. Because Willmoore and I were close friends and collaborators who spent the better part of our time together discussing the very matters analyzed in this book (as well as being of like mind in our thinking and approaches to the American tradition), the last four chapters are best read as a continuation of the first four. Though different stylistically, the theme and the thrust of the materials for which I bear primary responsibility are in keeping with our views of the American experience—views which are readily discernible in the Vanderbilt Lectures.

The exceptions to which I referred above would be these: First, the final chapter of this book contains a good deal of the material presented in the fifth Vanderbilt lecture. However, because it was an "extra" lecture, written on the spot under the pressures of time and circumstance, I felt less constrained (less, that is, than when dealing with the first four lectures) in editing or adding to it. Moreover, in light of the expansion of the lectures into book form, additions and changes of fairly substantial nature were definitely called for.

Second, wherever possible I have tried to incorporate Willmoore's thinking and views concerning the issues raised in the lectures and in my chapters. To this end I have gone over with great care lecture notes provided me by certain of Willmoore's better students at the University of Dallas, his writings pertaining to the matters raised in this book, and our personal correspondence.

Acknowledgments

Thanks are due many and for different reasons.

To the Board of Directors of the Relm Foundation of Ann Arbor and to Mr. Richard A. Ware for providing me the opportunity to complete this manuscript. Their understanding and generosity I will never forget.

To Yvona Kendall Mason and Mary Dyer, who spared no effort to put this book together. Thanks are not enough to express my profound gratitude for their hard work.

To James B. Williams (Louisiana State University), Ross Lence (Indiana University), Dennis Nolan (Harvard Law School), and Leo Paul de Alvarez (University of Dallas). Each in his own way made this a better book than it would have been otherwise. Special thanks are due to Professor Charles S. Hyneman of Indiana University. The short Appendix I to this book was inspired by his critique. Professor James McClellan of Hampden-Sydney College, who helped me understand the intricacies of the common law, is also due special thanks.

To Professor Avery Leiserson, who invited Willmoore Kendall to speak at Vanderbilt University.

To Professor Rocco Porreco, Dean of the Georgetown Graduate School, who allowed me to clutter up his offices and cause mayhem among his staff in order to complete the task at hand.

To Mr. Richard Wentworth, now of the University of Illinois Press, for his patience and understanding in the initial phases of this project.

To Mrs. Martha L. Hall of the Louisiana State University Press. She set me straight on matters of punctuation, spelling, style, and grammar.

To Nellie Cooper Kendall, who had the persistence to push the book through to completion.

To my wife Claire, for reasons that I shan't disclose.

Finally, to paraphrase Willmoore: Let us have no foolishness about their not being responsible for this book and its contents. All, in their own way, must bear some part of the responsibility.

The Basic Symbols
of the American
Political Tradition

CHAPTER I

What Is Traditional Amongst Us?

The central theme of this book is one that few, if any, historians or political theorists would have chosen to explore as recently as fifteen years ago. Indeed, nobody could have chosen it prior to two developments in the course of those fifteen years that have assuredly taken most students of American politics completely by surprise. To begin with we want to examine these two developments, dealing first with the simpler and more familiar of the two.

Up to a recent moment—just what moment we need not say precisely—the American political tradition did not constitute a problem, whereas today it does. Put otherwise: Up to a certain recent moment Americans did not raise questions about an American political tradition for the simple reason that everybody knew, or thought he knew, what the tradition was. In other words, everybody took it for granted that there was a traditional American way of self-government, a traditional American way of doing things politically, that reached back over the decades to the generation that produced the Declaration of Independence, the Constitution, the Federalist Papers, and the Bill of Rights. Put otherwise again: everyone took it for granted that underlying our traditional way of doing things politically was a traditional set of political principles or political beliefs that Americans, back over the decades, had cherished both because they were correct political principles, that is, principles that Americans *ought* to cherish, and because they were *ours*, bequeathed to us by *our* forefathers. And, here again, everyone assumed that these principles could be fully articulated without difficulty if and when the occasion arose to do so. Hence, the task of identifying and spelling out our basic political principles was far from being deemed a problem of importance by scholars, statesmen, or even the ordinary citizen. For example, when our great waves of immigration descended upon us at the turn of the century, and we suddenly faced the challenge of the "greenhorn," the newly-arrived immigrant from, for example, Eastern Europe, the greenhorn who spoke no English and had had no experience with anything remotely resembling American political principles, everybody seemed to know what needed to be done: namely, teach the greenhorn the English language (English, curiously, not American) which constituted the first step toward his Americanization, and then teach him Americanism, that is, the principles of our political system. Everyone seemed to agree, in other words, that there was such a thing as Americanism (that is, an American political tradition) and—a matter of great importance for us here—that Americanism *ought to be inculcated upon the immigrants.*[1] More: It was the *duty* of those immigrants to understand and cherish our political principles, and *our* duty to see to it that they did. And certainly everyone agreed that there could be no question about what ought to be said in the textbooks used in the Americanization schools. So, new Americans like Edward Bok were duly Americanized—indeed, Bok could and

---

1 This is admittedly quite different from what we find today. Witness only the argument often encountered to this effect: "Because we don't know what Americanism is, who can tell us what is un-American?" In the groves of academe, of course, such reasoning was frequently used to assail the House Un-American Activities Committee. We suspect that this might well have been the reason the name of the Committee was changed.

did call his autobiography *The Americanization of Edward Bok*.[2]

Today, by contrast, there certainly is a problem about the American political tradition, even though different commentators might differ in their formulations of that problem. One provisional formulation of the problem we can offer is this: Some amongst us are today saying things about the American political tradition, about the traditional American way of doing things politically, about the political principles that have the sanction of tradition in America, that others of us believe to be untrue. And this belief is bolstered because we have had, in the last few years, a sudden spate of books involving a kind of inquiry into the American political tradition that we had never before seen in America. Take, for example, Harold Hyman's *To Try Men's Souls*.[3] It concerns itself with the history of *loyalty* oaths in America, and the author arrives at the following conclusion (very disturbing of course to those who had been saying that loyalty oaths were somehow *un-*American) : In point of fact, loyalty oaths have figured prominently in the American political tradition; in point of fact, loyalty oaths were administered and defended, equally and unabashedly, by George Washington, by one of the authors of *The Federalist*, and by Abraham Lincoln. Nor, according to Hyman, is that all: Horrible though the fact be to contemplate, the very Declaration of Independence includes a loyalty oath, one moreover that our forefathers *administered* as a loyalty oath.[4] Or take, for another example, Leonard Levy's

---

2 Bok, *Americanization of Edward Bok* (New York: Scribner and Sons, 1920) .

3 Hyman, *To Try Men's Souls: Loyalty Tests in American History* (Berkeley: University of California Press, 1959) . The best commentary on Hyman's position is Charles S. Hyneman's "Conflict, Toleration and Agreement: Persisting Challenge for Democratic Government," The Edmund J. James Lecture, University of Illinois, 1962, *University of Illinois Bulletin*, No. 75 (1965) .

4 Indeed, the Constitution contains within it a loyalty oath that no President has yet refused to take.

The Legacy of Suppression.[5] It is concerned with the status of freedom of expression in the American past and arrives—with great reluctance on the part of the author—at the conclusion that the founders of the American republic certainly did not believe in freedom of speech and press as we today understand it. Their intention was that it should remain *ill*egal in the United States to speak ill of the government and its officials. Indeed, horrible as *that* fact may be to contemplate, the very idea that the individual citizen has a right to speak and write things that tend to bring the government into contempt was, according to Levy, unknown in America down to a date considerably later than 1789 (when, as you know, our Bill of Rights was written).

Both of these books, let us take care to note, were written by men whose research had brought them rude surprises—surprises, moreover, precisely about what *is* traditional politically in the United States. They were written by men who suddenly found themselves wishing, and wishing out loud, that the American past had been *different* from what it in fact was; by men, one might go so far as to say, who end up with the conclusion: The tradition, contrary to what we have been told, embodies *wrong* political principles, not right ones. That is an extremely interesting fact in itself, and one that we shall explore in some detail later. Our point here, however, is that the two books in question did not get themselves written until a very recent date, which is to say that people had for a long while been talking grandly about the American political tradition without knowing even the first things about it. Not

5 Originally published by Harvard University Press (1960), this book has been reprinted in the Harper Torchbook series. In the Harper edition, Levy answers certain criticisms of his work in his preface. This he does admirably. But here, as well as in his later work, *Jefferson and Civil Liberties: The Darker Side* (Cambridge, Mass.: Belknap Press of Harvard University Press, 1963), he is still unable to surmount his own libertarian prejudices which simply prevent him from comprehending or explaining to others the nature of that tradition which he does find through his own researches.

surprisingly, then, when someone at last took the trouble to go back and study the facts, the facts turned out to be different from what our publicists had been alleging them to be. In other words—which of course explains how these books came to be written when they did—a question was suddenly in the air, disturbing in the very nature of the case, that had not been there before, namely: What is traditional amongst us, politically, after all? Or, if you like, How much do we really know about the tradition? and, Hadn't we better go find out what has been traditional amongst us, find out what kind of thing it really was? All this (and many other examples could be cited) represents a new kind of inquiry amongst us, and shows that Americans are suddenly somehow disturbed about their political tradition, and disturbed about it in a way that is quite unprecedented. For the first time, to go no further, some Americans (as we have already intimated) are questioning our national habit of identifying the traditional with the good. For the first time, again, some Americans, a different set to be sure and a small one, are beginning to question whether there is an American political tradition at all, in the sense of a single set of political principles that the generality of Americans have in fact cherished through the long sweep of their history. That question is not, perhaps, yet being asked in a very clear or sophisticated manner, but it too is in the air, and we may be sure we have not heard the last of it.

Furthermore, we have yet to ask seriously, though this also some Americans are beginning to ask, What do we actually mean by "tradition" to begin with? Consequently, to go no further, we have no answer to the question: Suppose that the generality of Americans, at some mid-point between the Framers' time and ours, up and changed their minds about political principles in general, so what had been traditional up to that moment was replaced by something new, something therefore that is "traditional" only for recent decades? Must we, in such a case, cease to speak of *the* tradition? Must the traditional be understood as only that which reaches back over the decades to the beginnings? And, in any case, what in America *are* the beginnings? The Declaration of Independence, you say? Ah, but perhaps there was already a political tradition in America, even perhaps a very old tradition in America, when the Declaration was written; a tradition, moreover, that we must understand in order to understand the Declaration. And from all of this we can see at once that the American political tradition is now a problem where it was not a problem before. And we can also perceive precisely why that topic would not have occurred to anyone fifteen or twenty years ago; or, if you like, would not have been regarded as sufficiently problematic to merit the attention of the scholarly community.

Before moving along to the second development to which we referred earlier, let us pause to nail down and develop a little further what has been said up to this point. The *main* point is that we (meaning by "we" above all "we scholars," "we professionals in the field of political science") begin to discover that we are astonishingly *ignorant* about the American political tradition, this, moreover, on any showing you like as to what we mean by "tradition"; and that we have only just begun, in recent years, to do something about it—that is, to begin to make the studies, do the research, that might some day dispel our ignorance and make us knowledgeable.

This is *not* to say that we have no literature on the American political tradition. Such books as Vernon Parrington's *Main Currents*,[6] or Clinton Rossiter's *Seedtime of the Republic*,[7] come to mind at once. And we have other books, of

6 Parrington, *Main Currents in American Thought: An Interpretation of American Literature from the Beginnings to 1920* (2 vols.; New York: Harcourt, Brace, and Company, 1927, 1930) .

7 Rossiter, *Seedtime of the Republic* (New York: Harcourt, Brace, and Company, 1955) .

more or less the same sort, by Ralph Gabriel,[8] by Merle Curti,[9] and by a handful of other scholars one could name if one put one's mind to it. And the question arises, What can be said about these books in connection with the main point as stated above? Principally this: They tend to prove the main point rather than disprove it, because they are "thesis" books, question-begging books, whose authors pretty clearly "knew" all the answers before they began their research. The American political tradition, the books say with a single voice, is the tradition of "freedom" and "equality," the tradition of "rights of the individual," or, if you like, of the *natural* rights of the individual, as proclaimed by our Declaration of Independence and as glorified and protected by our Constitution and our Bill of Rights. But this, clearly, the authors do not learn, or even profess to learn, by consulting these documents; they know it before they pick them up. One might even say they pick up the documents only in order to spot passages that confirm, or seem to confirm, the thesis; and, in general, there has been no one to say them Nay. If there were difficulties about all that (and, as we shall see, the difficulties cry up at you once you get to thinking about it), none of the authors mentioned was about to call attention to them. Indeed, the safest guess is that the authors in question saw no difficulties, though they were aware that some of our ancestors (the New England theocrats,

[8] Gabriel, *The Course of American Democratic Thought: An Intellectual History since 1815* (New York: Ronald Press, 1940) and *Main Currents in American History* (New York: Appleton-Century Company, 1942).

[9] Among Curti's books: *The American Paradox: The Conflict of Thought and Action* (New Brunswick: Rutgers University Press, 1956); *Probing our Past* (New York: Harper and Bros., 1955), and *The Roots of American Loyalty* (New York: Columbia University Press, 1946). These works, along with those cited in footnote 8, above, constitute only a portion of that which we term throughout this volume "the official literature." James McGregor Burns, Robert A. Dahl, and Richard Hofstadter are today among the most prominent who accept the same framework of thinking and analysis. The "old timers" would include James Allen Smith, Charles Beard (at least in his earlier publications), and Albert Kales. We will have occasion to cite others in the following chapters.

for example) were certainly no friends of the rights of the individual, and they show that awareness by, so to speak, brushing them aside as a mere minority voice that has been silenced by the mainstream of the tradition. But no, we do *not* forget that we have a literature of the American political tradition, which has created the general intellectual atmosphere in which books like Hyman's on the loyalty oath, and Levy on freedom of expression, can seem so shocking (though few pay any attention to them).[10] And no, we do not forget either that that literature still rides high in our universities, and provides the ideological base for most of what we hear from our political commentators and our political pundits. But we are convinced that the days of its ascendancy are numbered and that the time has come to begin to talk very seriously about where we are going to be when the thesis of that literature finally comes crashing down, as, for reasons we have already begun to make clear, come crashing down it must (as a result of the re-examination of the whole business that is now under way). There are, to put the matter quite simply, too many questions—questions that now are being asked—that the literature cannot answer. Indeed, nobody can answer them because the necessary research and thinking have yet to be done, and because as the research *gets* done we have on our hands not more and simpler answers but more and more mysteries that need to be cleared up. Perhaps, therefore, it would be helpful if, before turning to that second development of recent years that helps explain our topic, we set forth specific examples of the kind of questions the literature (let us, for the sake of convenience and clarity, call it the official literature) cannot answer, though, to be sure, the time has come when they need answering.

(1) The Constitution was written in 1787 by the men we

10 When and if we do heed such literature, it is likely to be with the response of the kid who confronted "Shoeless" Joe Jackson: "Tell me it ain't so."

call our Framers, and went into effect in 1789. But also in 1789 the First Congress wrote, and sent forward for ratification by the states, the Bill of Rights. So much everybody knows, as he knows too that we, as a nation, have lived ever since under the Constitution as amended by the Bill of Rights. Ah! But everybody also has tucked off in the corner of his mind this further piece of what we are going to call *guilty* information, information about which one does not feel quite comfortable, information about which, by preference (conscious or unconscious), we have always preserved a discreet silence, namely: Those famous Framers were, almost to a man, *opposed* to the adoption of a Bill of Rights, agreed to the adoption of the Bill of Rights only very reluctantly, and saw the Bill of Rights go into effect with grave misgivings as to what its effect might be on the frame of government devised at Philadelphia.[11] That we know off in the corner of our minds, and one might have expected our scholars, the custodians of the lore of our tradition, to raise and answer the questions: *Why* were the Framers opposed to the Bill of Rights? What reasons did they give for opposing the Bill of Rights? Might they have been correct in opposing a Bill of Rights, in arguing, as argue they did, that a Bill of Rights was incompatible with the Philadelphia Constitution? Which *is* the American tradition—the political philosophy of the Framers, which opposed a Bill of Rights, or the principles of the amendmentities (so they were called) of 1789? The official literature has no answer to such questions because, for good

---

11 This we would not so much as guess from such books as: Zechariah Chafee, *Free Speech in the United States* (Cambridge, Mass.: Harvard University Press, 1941); Alexander Meiklejohn, *Political Freedom: The Constitutional Powers of the People* (New York: Harper, 1960); Edward Dumbauld, *The Bill of Rights and What It Means Today* (Norman: University of Oklahoma Press, 1957); and Robert A. Rutland, *The Birth of the Bill of Rights, 1776–1791* (Chapel Hill: Published for the Institute of Early American History and Culture by the University of North Carolina Press, 1955).

or ill, it has systematically avoided them. Yet they now become very important questions.

(2) The Declaration of Independence, with its references to the Creator, to the laws of nature and of nature's God, to Divine Providence, appears to be the declaration of a religious people, of, more specifically, a *Christian* people. The Constitution and the Bill of Rights, by contrast, have in them not one word that could not have been written, and subscribed to, by a people made up of atheists and agnostics.[12] The Declaration seems to be the declaration of a people who wish to make clear above all else their commitment to work the will of God; the Constitution and Bill of Rights seem to be the expressions of a people whose exclusive concern is with the things of this world. Now: What happened between 1776 and 1787? Did there take place some far-reaching shift in the religious sentiments of the American revolutionaries? If not, then, which *is* the American political tradition—the religious commitment of the Declaration, or the religious indifferentism of the Constitution and the Bill of Rights? Again, the official literature (which, we may note in passing, has never wasted much time or thought on the religious emphasis of the Declaration) has no answers. Yet, answers are certainly called for.

(3) The Declaration, we are told, speaks of "natural" rights, and even pauses a moment to list some of the natural rights with which all men are endowed by their Creator: specifically, the right, or rights, to life, to liberty, and to the pursuit of happiness. More: The Declaration proclaims that governments are instituted to protect men, *all* men presumably, in the enjoyment of their natural rights. Now: One might fairly have expected that the revolution-makers who wrote the Dec-

---

12 This fact is, mistakenly in our opinion, taken to mean by certain of our best natural law theorists that there can be no real dialogue or recourse to reason in the American system. See on this point a very provocative article by L. Brent Bozell, "The Death of the Constituiton," *Triumph*, III, No. 2 (February, 1968).

laration would, when their revolution had succeeded and the time had come for them to write a Constitution, take as their central problem: *What* rights must be protected? What form of government will best protect those rights? But, paradoxically, the Constitution says little about rights and their protection (and virtually nothing about what we today speak of as rights), and, curiously, the Bill of Rights itself tends to avoid the term "rights," and says nothing about how rights are to be protected (see the discussion in Chapter 7). The Constitution speaks—in its Preamble, where the question of what the new government is being instituted for is answered —not of rights, but of a whole series of purposes that are not present, even by implication, in the Declaration: a more perfect union, for example, and justice, the blessings of liberty, the general welfare, etc. Still another fact that most of us have not dwelt on is this: The Framers of the Constitution were often accused, through the period of 1787–89, of having betrayed the "spirit," that is one supposes, the principles of 1776. And again the questions, once you look a second time, crowd in on us. How do we explain the sudden disappearance, between 1776 and 1787, of natural rights, and of the problem of how natural rights are to be protected? Had the American people changed their minds, somewhere along the line, about *the* great issue over which, for so we are told, the Revolutionary War had been fought? In any case, which *is* the tradition, natural rights and their protection? Or the ends of government as set forth in the Preamble of the Constitution? The best answer the official literature has for us is that the Bill of Rights was devised precisely to repair an "oversight" on the part of the Framers. But clearly this answer will not do. The *fact* is that the Philadelphia Convention heard, and unanimously voted down, a last-minute attempt to bring the Constitution into line with the Declaration on this point. Why? The official literature has no answer.

(4) The Declaration asserts flatly that "all men are created equal" and makes the resultant "all equal men" the subjects of those natural rights of which we were just speaking. Equality, we are told, *is* therefore one of the basic principles of the American political tradition and we are, in consequence, committed as a nation *to* equality. Yet the Constitution says nothing of equality, and neither, rather surprisingly, does the Bill of Rights (unless just possibly by implication) —and this despite the fact that the Preamble offered the Framers every opportunity *to* include equality as one of the goods the new frame of government was to assure.[13] Equality just disappears from our political vocabulary, disappears as the ink dries on the Declaration of Independence, and is not heard of again, to all intents and purposes, until Abraham Lincoln reminds his contemporaries of the language of the Declaration and begins to insist that America has failed to live up to one of its deepest commitments (though Lincoln himself turns out to have understood by the word equality some rather curious things). And when equality finally reappears in a great public document it does so in the form not of equality simply, but equal protection of the laws, which neither that generation nor the two subsequent generations appear to have interpreted as a promise of equality, at least not equality of the kind that our Supreme Court now seems ready to champion. The question cannot be sidestepped. What *is* the American political tradition? Is it a tradition that exalts equality as one of the goods of the good society, or a tradition that, like the Constitution and the Bill of Rights, conspicuously avoids the topic of equality—and, in avoiding it, seems to repudiate the Declaration of Independence commitment? Is the American political tradition the tradition of the textbooks, which indeed situates the "all men are equal" clause at the center of our political experience, or is it the tradition of

13 See our discussion below, principally Chaps. 5 through 7.

American life as it is actually lived and thus a tradition of inequality? The official literature this time does have an answer, namely: The tradition is equality; but, as we have seen, that answer will not bear confrontation with the facts, not even with the facts that are most notorious.[14]

(5) The men who made the American Revolution, we have all been brought up to believe, were in fact conservatives, not revolutionaries or even patriots.[15] As Edmund Burke put it, they were fighting for the traditional rights of Englishmen, were therefore fighting for the best interests of England itself. Concretely, we are told, the slogan of the Revolution was "No Taxation Without Representation." And the implication here is that Englishmen had been being born for centuries with a right not to be taxed by a government in which they were not represented, despite the fact that millions of Englishmen were not admitted to the vote, that is, to being represented in Parliament, until the present century. Now: Nothing is more natural, after the fact of a war, than for the historians on each side to concoct the prettiest story possible about the purpose for which that side shed its blood (and spilled that of its opponents), though to a considerable degree that is precisely what has *not* happened in this case. Burke's interpretation of the American Revolution, perhaps because it lent itself to the designs of the democratizing forces in England, pretty much prevailed on yon side of the Atlantic too (and is reflected in the bad conscience the English, in general, have shown during the recent world crisis of so-called colonialism). Nothing is more natural, either, than for the heirs of a revolution to try, soon after it is over, to wrap it in the mantle of a tradition. Nevertheless the idea that the American revolution-

---

14 See Chap. 5.

15 Such a view is so widely held that we cannot possibly cite all those who maintain it. We do know that Daniel Boorstin was one of the first to maintain the notion with some success. See his *The Genius of American Politics* (Chicago: University of Chicago Press, 1953).

aries were fighting for their rights as Englishmen begins, like
the other theses we have been examining, to crumble under
the impact of new and factual research—for example, that of
John Miller of Stanford, whose book[16] on the years leading
up to the Revolution has become a "must" reading for all
students of American history. Our point here, however, is
merely that there are questions in the air that the official literature simply cannot answer: If our ancestors were fighting
for their traditional rights as Englishmen, as we are told, then
we are entitled to be told *what* traditional rights of Englishmen, and to be shown that Englishmen had in fact traditionally enjoyed those rights—as, also, we are entitled to be told
what happened to those rights after the Revolution was over.
Are they, for example, the same rights that were in due course
written into the Bill of Rights? If so, then why—the question,
you notice, keeps on bobbing up—why were the Framers reluctant to embody them in their new constitution? And, in
any case, if we wish to know the purpose for which the Revolution was fought, why not do the obvious thing and go to the
revolutionaries' own statement as to what they were up to,
that is, to the Declaration of Independence as a whole and not
to this or that phrase, wrenched out of context, that happens
to lend itself to a particular interpretation of the Revolution. Again: What are we to make of the fact that the agitators
who whipped up the first ardor of the revolutionaries, those
agitators (like Sam Adams and Tom Paine) to whom the official historians go for quotes to support their thesis, disappear
from American history in the course of the war, and that the
war turned for its actual leadership to another breed of men
altogether—a breed of men who precisely did *not* talk loosely
about "rights?" Finally, a question that the official historians
tend to avoid like the plague, what about the rights of the

16 Miller, *Origins of the American Revolution* (Stanford University Press,
1957) .

American Tories, who were silenced, persecuted, robbed and, finally, driven across the border into Canada like so many cattle? They were "all men" too, but where were the famous natural rights when *they* needed them? Don't misunderstand us: Our purpose is not at all to "debunk" the American revolutionaries, toward whom we feel a reverence that we are willing to place beside that of any Chinese traditionalist meditating on his ancestors. Our point, as it has been all along, is that there are too many questions the official literature cannot answer, and especially the big question we always end up with, namely: What *is* the American political tradition? Is it, back beyond 1776, a matter of the traditional rights of Englishmen—so that as we trace the tradition back from our day to its beginnings, it so to speak crosses the Atlantic in 1776 and earlier than that can best be studied not in America but in England? Or should we, in tracing it back, keep to this side of the Atlantic? Might it be that in 1776 there was already a highly developed *American* (American, not English) political tradition, hazy perhaps on some points but crystal-clear on others, of which the Declaration of Independence is a natural expression precisely because the rights it claims are, if we may put it so, the rights not of Englishmen but of Americans? Might the notion of the Declaration of Independence as the beginning for the American tradition—for that is what it becomes in the official version of our history—be false? and false in the two-fold sense that it conceals (*a*) the Americanness of the Declaration and (*b*) the truly revolutionary character of the steps taken in 1776 and 1787, so inviting us to miss the point about what really happened through those crucial eleven years? These are the important questions that you should keep in mind as we proceed.

We come now to the second of the two recent developments that account for the topic we have chosen, namely: the eruption, into the vocabulary and intellectual apparatus of political philosophy, of such concepts as *symbols, symbolization, symbolic forms;* and of such related concepts as *myths, constitution of being, the self-interpretation of a political society, representation,* etc. This, as far as American political science is concerned, is mainly a matter of the sudden impact upon our political thought of the writings of Professor Eric Voegelin, whose major works have been signed from the Louisiana State University Press.[17] To put the matter in its briefest and simplest terms: Professor Voegelin has fixed attention upon what, for most of us who have come under his influence, is a wholly new dimension of political experience and thus of political analysis. And he has set us off, as political scientists, on a new kind of task, specifically, the identification and understanding of the symbols and myths that "represent" the American people in their experience as a political society. This is not to suggest that the key words we have used—by way of edging into the problem—were wholly new when Voegelin began to write. American political scientists had long been aware, of course, that symbols—for example, the flag, the Great Seal, the slogan *e pluribus unum,* perhaps even the slogan "In God We Trust"—had some kind of role in politics, and precisely as symbols to which political orators might appeal in their attempts to sway the hearts and minds of their fellow citizens. They had also been aware that, somewhere along the way in our study of politics, we must take into account something called *myths,* that is, tales about the past, most particularly perhaps tales about our national heroes of the past, that the people tell over and over again to themselves and, without regard to their historicity, believe to be *true* tales that, besides being true, embody an important "lesson" or "moral," which people are perhaps less likely to violate

17 Voegelin, *Order and History:* Vol. I, *Israel and Revelation;* Vol. II, *The World of the Polis;* Vol. III, *Plato and Aristotle* (Baton Rouge: Louisiana State University Press, 1956, 1957, 1957). Also, *The New Science of Politics* (Chicago: University of Chicago Press, 1952).

because of its embodiment in a cherished myth. The tale about George Washington and the cherry tree, for example, was such a tale, there to remind us that the Father of Our Country, he who was First in the Hearts of his Countrymen, already as a little boy stood committed to Truth. And little boys who hear the tale will necessarily take to heart the noble precept "I Cannot Tell a Lie," will recognize it as pointing up the same moral as "Thou Shalt Not Bear False Witness" that they learn at Sunday School, and will, in consequence, be better patriots because of associating the nation George Washington founded, *their* nation, the United States, with a central teaching of *their* religion, Christianity. So much, so to speak, was in the air when Voegelin began to write, but the political scientists who spoke of such things as symbols and myths did so—naturally enough no doubt given the prevailing intellectual mood—as part of their general self-imposed task of identifying the role of the *irrational* in politics. They themselves, being "scientists," were not, of course, about to be taken in by such things as myths and symbols; myths and symbols were regarded primarily as ploys by which the smart people "manipulated" the stupid people, who because of their stupidity could only be appealed to on the level of irrationality. Part of the task of the political scientist—and some may recall the efforts of Thurman Arnold in this connection—was to spot such symbols and myths and try to understand how they "work," [18] the extent to which they do indeed make people's hearts go pit-a-pat and do affect people's otherwise incomprehensible "behavior." (It is interesting to notice, in passing, that the major proposal in Mr. Thurman Arnold's major book in this area was the proposal that our society be operated in the future by, of course, people in the know about

[18] Arnold, *The Symbols of Government* (New Haven: Yale University Press, 1935) and *The Folklore of Capitalism* (New Haven: Yale University Press, 1937).

such things as symbols and myths, like a well-run insane asylum, where the big job is simply to make all the inmates as comfortable as possible under the rather dreadful circumstances.) Thus, one may fairly say that the American political scientists before Voegelin who spoke of myths and symbols certainly did not take the myths and symbols as such seriously: Symbols and myths as such were by definition nonsensical, though because nonsensical a very serious business—as, for the psychiatrist, the delusions of Miss DeHaviland in the snake-pit are a very serious business. Moreover, one may fairly say that those who spoke of myths and symbols in those days tacitly assumed that myths and symbols differed among themselves *only* as regards their *effectiveness* for purposes of manipulation, so that—and this is the main point—one did not ask whether, for example, this myth was true in some sense in which that myth was false, or whether this symbol was meaningful in some sense in which that symbol could be shown to be empty of meaning, or, above all perhaps, whether this cluster of symbols or myths was beneficent in its workings while that cluster was maleficent in its workings. Indeed the political scientists in question were, in general, men who denied that the political scientist has any proper concern with such matters as beneficence (who is to say what is beneficent?), or meaningfulness (isn't meaningfulness a matter of opinion, and isn't one man's opinion as good as another's?), or even truth (except, if you like, the "scientific" truth of the laboratory and the table of statistics).[19]

To all that kind of thing Eric Voegelin, from the first moment of his appearance on the scene, said: "Not so." The task of political analysis *begins*, he teaches, with each people's attempts at *self-interpretation*, at *self-understanding*, as a po-

19 This is true, we conjecture, because most of these political scientists were greatly influenced by the "behaviorists" or, if not that, were weaned on John Stuart Mill's *On Liberty*.

litical society. And peoples, he points out as a matter of *historical fact (each* people in the course of constituting itself as a political society), soon raise with themselves, and attempt to answer, the questions: Who am I? What am I here for? Where do I fit in the *constitution of being*— in the whole complicated business of gods and goddesses, of good and evil spirits, of life and death and successive generations, of men and animals and insects and plants? What do I assert as *true,* as *good,* as *meaningful,* as *beautiful?* These, Voegelin teaches, are questions that *no* people constituting itself as a political society can sidestep, questions that do arise as a matter of course, in the process by which (in Rousseau's phrase) a people *becomes* a people, that is, gets itself politically organized for action in history (if, that is, it be a people aware—for not all peoples are—that there is such a thing as history) ; or, if not for action in history, then for action simply, since act a people must as it becomes and lives its life as a people and chooses between alternative courses of action. So that, even beyond these questions, there always lie the further questions: How do I—this people—decide what to do? To what standards do I refer my decisions *as* to what to do? By what procedures am I to decide what to do, and on which persons or types of persons in my bosom am I to rely when I make such decisions? All these, says Voegelin, are questions to which *all* peoples give, have to give, some kind of answer, even if the answer be refusal to answer (which is itself, curious as that may seem, a kind of answer). Now, according to Voegelin, peoples typically answer these questions precisely through the development of symbols and myths. Hence, political philosophy, as most political scientists understand the term, is a tardy development in the history of a people, and, moreover, a development precisely out of the stuff of symbols and myths. The symbols and myths become, therefore, the *first* order of business for the political scientist; and, in the first instance at least, the myths and symbols are to be taken seriously above all else in politics.

To put this another way, Eric Voegelin has taught us that what we are in the habit of calling the political *tradition* of a people is above all a matter of its self-interpretation (from moment to moment, from decade to decade, from century to century) from the beginning to the end of its existence as a people. It is a matter, therefore, of a people's own understanding of its place in the *constitution of being* and of its *role in history*, of what it calls upon itself to be and do as it lives its life as a political society—a matter, in short, of the *symbols* by which it represents or interprets itself to itself. And that, Voegelin teaches us further, is above all a matter of the way a people symbolizes, pictures to itself, its relation to, as he puts it, transcendent truth, that is, the truth of the soul and the truth of society, as apprehended by Western man in the course of, first, his religious experience, and, second, his experience in the realm of philosophy. All societies think of themselves, once they begin to think of themselves at all, as representing a truth, a meaning, about the nature and destiny of man, and thus about that which, in the constitution of being, is above and beyond man. Man in society, Voegelin emphasizes, in fact *always* asserts, never fails to assert, a relationship, even if only the negative relationship of denial, to that which is above and beyond him, and thus transcendent.[20] (We may speak of the negative relationship of denial when man in society sets himself up as that which is the highest in the constitution of being, as men in some societies have done.) Political societies no doubt begin as mere external facts, that is, as this or that segment of humankind who are "represented" by a ruler or a set of rulers—represented in the sense that they in fact obey commands emanating from a recognizable source

20 See in particular Voegelin's *The New Science of Politics*.

of authority, which does, as a matter of fact, act for that segment of mankind in its relations with other segments of mankind with respect to such matters as war, commerce, and the like. But, as Voegelin points out, soon or late man in society shows himself unwilling to leave it at that: Regimes that are *merely* external relations of command and obedience are, we perceive, inherently unstable and short-lived; thus, a moment inevitably comes in the life of any emergent society when it begins to think of itself as what Voegelin terms a little *world of meaning* all its own, with such and such a relation to the other little worlds of meaning around it, and to a *great* world of meaning of which all the little worlds of meaning are merely parts. For the human beings within each little world of meaning, the meaning for it becomes, to use Voegelin's vocabulary, the "mode and condition" of their self-realization as human beings; or, as another great political philosopher of our day would put it,[21] it becomes their regime, their way of life, illuminated for them in due course by rites and myths, symbolic in character, that express their relation as human beings first to each other, then to the political authority whose commands they obey, and then, finally, to that, be it God or higher law or the music of the spheres, which is above and beyond all human beings. "The self-illumination of society through symbols," writes Voegelin, "is an integral part of social reality, and one may say even its essential part; for through such symbolization the members of a society experience it as more than an accident or a convenience; they experience it as of their human essence."[22] Or again: "Every human society has an understanding of itself through a variety of symbols." Or still again: when political science goes to work on a given society, "It will inevitably start from the rich body of

21 We refer here, of course, to Leo Strauss.
22 Voegelin, *The New Science of Politics*, 27.

self-interpretation of [the] society and proceed by critical clarification of . . . [its] symbols." [23]

A few further points, and we shall have followed Voegelin
about as far as we need to for our purposes. First this point:
A people that has given itself a set of symbols does not just
leave it at that. With the passing of time it develops its symbols; perhaps enriching or impoverishing them, perhaps giving them new twists, perhaps emphasizing this symbol at the
expense of that one, or even perhaps dropping old symbols
and replacing them with new ones. The original symbols are
likely, Voegelin teaches us, to be *compact,* that is, compressed,
by comparison with that which they will become with the
passing of time—by which we may understand him to mean
that the original symbols hold within themselves the potentiality of development, unpredictable development one may
add, in this direction or that one—much as the child is a *compact* version of the man that he is to become, and becomes
that man by developing this potentiality or that one in this
way or that. Put otherwise, the original symbols are full of
alternative possible meanings which in due course may be
seized upon, now this one and now that one, and developed.
Voegelin calls the process by which the alternative meanings
separate off from the original symbols, *differentiation,* a process the understanding of which is indispensable for our subsequent analysis of the American tradition.

Second: In Western Civilization basic symbolizations tend
to be variants of the original symbolization of the Judaeo-
Christian religious tradition: variants, this is to say, of the tale
according to which a *founder,* Moses, leads the people out of
the realm of darkness, *Egypt,* into the *desert* (the essential
meaning of which is that it is *not* Egypt, but a place from
which the people can move in any of a thousand directions,
including back to Egypt, and must, because it no longer has

23 *Ibid.,* 28.

the Egyptians to tell it what to do, *choose* a direction) toward a Promised Land, which it becomes the business of a people, through its action, to conquer or achieve or build (as the case may be). (The Old Testament symbolism, with which all of us are of course familiar, is Voegelin's favorite example of what we mean by the *compactness* of an original set of symbols—as the history of the Jews, and their successive experiments with alternative meanings of the symbols, is the prime illustration of what he means by differentiation.) In the desert, we must notice further, the Founder, or Founders, give (s) the people its political regime or order, including the basic rules by which it is to move toward the Promised Land.,

Third: We must not, when we stand in the presence of an original or compact set of symbols, look for what we fashionably call political *principles;* the principles come only later, as a result of what Voegelin calls critical clarification of the symbols—or, if you like, as a result of what happens to the symbols when political philosophers and pundits go to work on them, and spell out their content in what we may call *propositional* form. The critical clarification, which may be skillful or unskillful, faithful to the original symbols or unfaithful to them, etc., comes later, after the symbols, but always proceeds with the symbols as its raw material.

Fourth and finally: Voegelin gives us no rules by which to proceed with this new kind of analysis of a political society. There are no rules to tell us where to begin or what precisely to look for as we seek to understand a political society in terms of its representative symbols. Nor are there rules to tell us when we have got hold of the symbols that do in fact represent a society to itself, do in fact illuminate, for the members of a society, the meaning of that society, do in fact constitute the mode and condition of their self-realization. At first glance the absence of such rules might seem an insurmountable barrier to the fruitful implementation of this form of analysis.

However, two rules do suggest themselves on the basis of
Voegelin's own practice: (*a*) We must try to begin at the
beginning, lest we mistake some more or less differentiated
variant of the basic symbolization for the basic symbolization
itself. (Voegelin, for instance, is careful to go back beyond
the Convenant at Mount Sinai to the Covenant between God
and Abraham, from what we might call the myth of Moses to
the myth of Abraham.) Now this, as we have already intimated, poses great problems as we approach the American political experience, where we cannot easily say that this or that
is the beginning. And a further complication is this: We must
be very careful not to begin before the beginning, that is,
with a set of symbols put forward at a moment before the people begins to constitute itself as a people. To avoid this pit-
fall, we must show some kind of historical continuity between
the beginning that we seize upon and that much later moment at which the people is in fact constituted as a people for
action in history. This, of course, will also take some thinking
about in any analysis of the American tradition. (*b*) A second,
though implicit, rule is this: We must never lose sight, over
and above the symbols upon which we are fixing attention, of
our people's *action*; that is, what it in fact does as compared,
or contrasted, with what we would expect it to do given this or
that set of symbols that it seems to have put forward in the
course of its attempts at self-interpretation. Put otherwise:
Unless we can see a *correspondence* between the symbols we
have in hand and the people's action in history, the symbols
we have in hand do not in fact represent that people, and we
must look a second time for the symbols that do in fact represent them.

   With these two rules in mind we are prepared to ask, Where
in America *is* the beginning? The official literature, as yet un-
influenced by the mode of analysis set forth here, answers this
question roughly along the following lines: The beginning

is the Declaration of Independence, which is the moment at which the American people begins to speak as a people and to constitute itself as a people. In a larger and more encompassing sense, the beginning is the Founding Fathers, the Framers, who first wrote the Declaration of Independence, which is their statement of principles in the war they fought for their traditional rights as Englishmen, then wrote the Constitution in which they laid down our frame of government, then wrote *The Federalist*, in which they explicated the Constitution, then wrote the Bill of Rights, in which, by way of repairing an oversight, they spelled out the rights that our frame of government was instituted to protect. Thus, while the beginning is the Declaration of Independence, we also stand in the presence of what may aptly be termed the Myth of the Framers, and in the presence of a cluster of symbols—Declaration of Independence, Constitution, Federalist Papers, Bill of Rights—which *are* for many people *the* basic symbols of the American political tradition, representative as a matter of course because all four have been adopted, as nothing else has been adopted, by the American people (one of them by tacit ratification in a war fought in its name; two of them by formal process' of ratification; one of them, *The Federalist,* by tacit elevation to the plane of authoritative Scripture). But even more than being adopted as basic symbols, they have been acted upon, so we are told, by the American people.

Why do we label this a myth? For a number of reasons. For one thing because it plays a recognizably mythical kind of hanky-panky with the heroes it holds up for our admiration by concretely lumping together as Framers or Founding Fathers the actors in four separate and distinct operations. Stated another way, once having identified the symbols that constitute the beginning, there is something more than a slight tendency to attribute their origins to one source (Framers or Founding Fathers) which necessitates the lumping to which we have referred. However, as a matter of historical fact, we know better than this. Thomas Jefferson, who did indeed write the draft of the Declaration of Independence, was not present at Philadelphia; one of the authors of *The Federalist,* Hamilton, played at Philadelphia a role not unlike that the Mets once played in the National League. The original proponents of the Bill of Rights were men who actually walked out of the Philadelphia Convention. And most of the miscellaneous writings of Thomas Jefferson that are held up to us as part of the wisdom of the Founding Fathers played *no* role in the founding, if by founding we mean founding, because they are dated long after the founding was completed.

Second, it is a myth because purely aside from the hanky-panky about the Fathers it is an obvious oversimplification, not to say prettification, of the sequence of historical events it putatively summarizes. For example, no lad-of-a-boy learning the tale at school would ever guess—and this bears repetition because it is so highly important—that the historical Framers, who did in fact frame the Consitution, opposed the very idea of a Bill of Rights. And this opposition, as we see from *The Federalist,* was deep-seated.

Third, it is a myth because it was in fact invented after the fact, and invented for a purpose that myth-makers often address themselves to in myth-making enterprises, namely: to get across a point that the actual historical record, the story as it actually happened, is likely to obscure or refute. For instance we are told that the four great documents, the symbols that the myth venerates, follow upon one another as logically and sense-makingly as the seasons of the year: We the people, acting through our representatives the Framers wrote the Declaration, which is precisely the kind of Declaration you would expect from us the people who will in due course write the Constitution; and the Constitution is just the Constitution that we who gave ourselves the Declaration would naturally have written. More: The Constitution would not have been adopted (another point, by the way, that seems about to go down the drain as a result of current research) but for its faithful explication and brilliant defense in *The Federalist;* and the Bill of Rights was just what we needed in order to round out the whole business and bring the Constitution fully in line with the Declaration of Independence. All of this makes a nice, tidy package and is precisely what our official literature disposes us to believe.

Fourth, it is a myth because it has a way of surviving which is like that of a myth. It is believed and cherished quite without regard to its historicity; believed and cherished with the kind of passion that myths engender; believed and cherished, finally, by persons who, quite naturally, share the purposes of those who originally invented it.

Finally, and most important, it is a myth because like that of most typical American myths, it spins itself out of nothingness: The hero rides into town out of a vaguely eastern nowhere (those rights of Englishmen, who from the vantage point of the Liberty Bell are indeed East), already possessed of the qualities he is to show at High Noon, unexplained, unaccounted for, without even an immediate past, so that we don't know where he was yesterday or the day before, when and how he learned to "draw"—learned to draw so quickly or shoot so straight—or who taught him the lofty principles by which, before riding off into the setting sun, he does justice in the course of the day. If, of course, we look too closely—too closely in either case—we realize that before the beginning the myth holds out to us there must have been an earlier beginning—and unless we have surrendered to the myth, we shall want to go behind its beginning to learn more about the hero. Most exponents of the myth, as we might well expect, do not look too closely. But we must do so if ever we are to answer the question, Where, in America, *is* the beginning?

CHAPTER II

In the Beginning:
The Mayflower Compact

The answer to the question "Where, in America, *is* the beginning?" is not easy to come by, but there is one approach that holds out great promise. Following Voegelin's prescriptions we should (*a*) keep to this side of the Atlantic, (*b*) remain within the same genre or literary category as the Declaration, the Constitution, and the Bill of Rights—namely, that of the public documents that have at least the look of ventures in self-interpretation by a political society, and (*c*) see what evidence we come across, if any, of a continuity among them. Having done this we will be in a position to see if there is any continuity in our political tradition and, more importantly, whether the Declaration of Independence and the Constitution are themselves continuous as a part of this tradition. This approach is suggested with the following exciting possibility in mind: The Declaration, seen in continuity with the earlier documents, may take on a new (though new only because forgotten) meaning. Now, in order to keep the matter relatively simple as well as non-controversial, we will for this purpose fix our attention on the four documents of this general character that turn up oftenest—for reasons that usually go unexplained—in the readings-books compiled by the high priests of the official literature, namely: the Mayflower Compact, the General Orders of Connecticut; The Body of Liberties of Massachusetts Bay, and the Virginia Declaration of

Rights. Let us read these documents with Voegelin's preoccupation in mind, and see what we come up with.

First, the Mayflower Compact.[1]

The scene, let us remind ourselves, is the saloon of the Mayflower, and the time just before the colonists go ashore to begin their new life (the precise year, of course, 1620). Now: The first thing we notice, perhaps to our surprise, perhaps not, is that the first words of the Compact, that is, the first words of the first political document ever composed in this hemisphere, borrow from the first words of Western man's traditional Christian invocation: "In the name of God," it reads, "Amen"—not, to be sure, "In the name of the Father, the Son, and the Holy Ghost, Amen" but that is perhaps all to the good for the purposes of the new commonwealth, since there will come a day when at least some of the heirs of the Compact would find "In the name of God, Amen" acceptable, but would take vigorous exception to any reference to the Trinity. That must be our first point: The one God is called to witness the compact that is about to be made. And we may safely assume that none of the signers of this *oath* is taking the matter lightly. Any subsequent violation of the oath will be no mere breaking of a promise but an offense against God, which suggests that the oath has been *discussed* at length before acquiring its present form. One might say that the signers, as if anticipating the town meeting that is to become the central ritual of New England politics, are as they *take* the oath sitting as a *deliberative assembly*—weighing and criticizing each word as it goes into the document, weighing and criticizing each word until *the* word is found that expresses what will later be called in America the sense of the meeting. We

[1] We have used for the source of our quotations Benjamin Perley Poore (ed.), *The Federal and State Constitutions, Colonial Charters and other Organic Laws of the United States* (Washington: Government Printing Office, 1877), I, 931. All future references to Poore are either to Vol. I or Vol. II of this work.

search the document in vain, therefore, for any hint that here
at the end of the deliberation there is any dissident or group
of dissidents whose signature is affixed reluctantly. The signers, one might say, put us on warning that they have thought
about the step they are taking, know what they are doing,
understand each other about what they are doing, and agree
about what they are doing.

From that point the document falls naturally into the following parts: (*a*) a part in which the signers identify themselves, say who they are; (*b*) a part in which they state the
purposes for which they undertake the business in hand; (*c*)
a part that contains an oath creating the body politic; and
(*d*) an addendum to the oath, in which the signers clarify
their obligations under the oath, letting us know what kind of
thing the new body politic is to be—and indicating to us, perhaps, what they understand the good body politic to be. We
have before us with these four parts a compact or undifferentiated form of the basic outline of the Constitution of the
United States, and of all other American constitutions: first
the identification of who is speaking, then the Preamble or
statement of purposes, then the specification of the body politic and of the subscribers' mutual obligations. As for (*a*),
the signers identify themselves as loyal subjects of the British
king, who is both the "dread Sovereign Lord" and "Defender of the Faith, etc.," where even the *etc.* seems to have its
significance. Further titles could have been added, but they
are not; the signers are content to pause, in the list of the
king's titles, once they have made it clear that the king to
whom they declare their allegiance is a king who, above all,
defends the *faith*. And we do not overburden the language before us when we recognize, in the phrase "Loyal Subjects," an
act of submission to the *laws* of the realm (this is not, not
consciously at least, a Declaration of Independence; nor, to anticipate a subsequent controversy in political philosophy, are

these men without law) . As for (b) , let us attend carefully to the purposes of the covenant as the signers list them. This "first Colony" in the northern parts of Virginia (amusingly enough, the signers don't know exactly where they are) is being planted for, first, "the Glory of God," second, the "Advancement of the Christian faith," and third, the "Honour of our King and Country," that is, for the honour of King James and Great Britain. And, if we look a bit further we find still a fourth purpose, namely: The signers combine themselves into a body politic not only for the furtherance of the ends already named, but also for "our better Ordering," that is, for the building of a *good* order (since the idea of its good is implicit in the word "better") —so that the door is thrown wide open for continuous deliberation about what is good order, what is good regime. Moreover, political order is placed on notice, as you will find it being done today in our Pledge of Allegiance, that it *must* be good political order, must justify itself as good and as serving the purposes named, or, failing that, get busy and improve itself (it is almost as if the signers were anticipating the 1787 decision that the political order of the Articles of Confederation had proved a disappointment, would not serve the purpose of a better ordering of us the people, and must therefore be replaced with a better order) . Then the first part of the oath: We the signers "solemnly" (again the emphasis that the act is a *deliberate* act, an act, let us say now, of deliberation) and "in the Presence of God" (the signers are, to be sure, repeating themselves, but the point seems to them worth emphasizing: God is their witness) do "covenant and combine [themselves] together into a civil body politic" for three purposes named, and, as we already know, a fourth, namely, "better Ordering." Then the second part of the oath: We covenant—the words we are about to read are truly breathtaking—to "enact, constitute, and frame such *just and equal Laws,* Ordinances, Acts, Constitutions, and Offices, as from time to time shall be thought most meet and convenient for the *general good of the Colony*," [2] *and* promise "all due Submission and Obedience" to these laws.

That is quite a mouthful, and we had best chew it a bit at a time: We the signers, the Compact says, combine in a civil body politic (not, let us note, simply a body politic, but a *civil body politic*) dedicated to the glorification of God (who witnesses our covenant), the advancement of the faith (which our king defends), the honour of our king and country, and, finally, to good order. Next: Within that civil body politic, and in virtue of this covenant, we undertake to frame just and equal laws, not simply laws, and great emphasis falls certainly on just and equal—any and all just and equal laws that shall be "thought [to be] most meet and convenient for the general Good of the Colony...." Again we must pause to take up this matter in easy stages: The laws are to address themselves to the *general good* of the colonies, and general good seems to figure here as a shorthand statement of the four purposes named: The laws are to be just and equal laws—that is, are to be just laws that apply equally to all. And again the door is thrown wide open to future deliberation on the question: What *is* just?—and thrown open the more certainly because the promise to obey, when we look a second time, is severely circumscribed: The obedience promised is not obedience simply, but *due* obedience and only to—let us note carefully—*just and equal* laws that are *thought* meet and convenient for the general good, something which we can understand fully only when we recognize that the words "as shall be thought" might conceivably have been left out but were not.

Let us think hard about that for a moment: We the signers promise due obedience, that is, that amount and kind of obedience that we in fact owe; how much and what kind of obedience is clearly left to some extent open (as it has been ever

---

2 Emphasis added.

since in America) as also is the question of what laws are just
and equal and meet and convenient for the general good of
the colony. And when we examine the text carefully we see
that it is not a matter of the laws *being* meet and convenient
but of their being *thought*—that is considered, deemed—meet
and convenient, which makes it a very complicated business:
Meetness and convenience, for the general good is not treated
as a settled matter, call for continuous thought and, we may
add, for new decisions. The new decisions, we are told, are to
be taken "from time to time"; meetness and convenience,
then, to come back to what we have seen increasingly to be
the central point, are a matter that calls for future deliberations like the one the signers have just taken. We the signers
will, we are saying, keep on deliberating about what is for the
general good; we the signers accept that—it is as old as Aristotle—as the standard to which we must subordinate our deliberations; but decisions do have to be made about the matter
from time to time, and the best we can hope for at any moment
is not laws that *are* meet and convenient to the purpose named
but laws *thought* to be that. What we promise to obey, then,
off in the future, is the results, fallible and subject to revision
as a matter of course, of future deliberations of a certain kind—
so that, if, off in the future, one of us the signers is to take exception to a law on the grounds that it is not for the general
good, not meet and convenient, he will be told: We did not
promise laws that *are* meet and convenient, but only such
laws as are *thought* to be; it is enough if a given law reflects
the general thinking amongst us as to what is meet and convenient; it is that which you have promised to obey. Then—
for we are now at the end of the document—a final sentence,
which hammers home the idea that we are "signers"; that is,
we have subscribed our names, as if by anticipation of the Declaration of Independence and the Constitution as reenactments of a deliberation followed by an act of signing, and the

date, This Year of Our Lord, 1620, so spelled out as to situate the signing as an event in the history of successions to the British Crown *and* as an event in the history of the Christian World (this latter, by the way, will be reenacted in the Constitution of the United States, which is also signed in a Year of Our Lord, though it does not otherwise mention God).

So much, then, for the language of the Mayflower Compact. We have as yet said nothing about whether it is or is not the act of founding of American political society. That we must decide in due course, in terms of the continuity we discover, if any, between it and the American politics we know. But we can for the moment pretend that it is the original act of founding, and make some comments that would be apposite if it were that.

First: the nascent society that interprets itself in the Compact is in some sense a religious, more specifically a Christian, society, which calls God in as Witness to its act of founding— nay, more, founds itself in His name. The society dedicates itself, from the moment of its founding, to (among other things) the glorification of God and the advancement, that is, one supposes, the development and propagation, of the Christian faith. So much is abundantly clear—or, if you like, it is clear that both the glorification of God and the advancement of the faith acquire, in the Compact, the status of *symbols*. But also, as Voegelin would have us expect, they are *compact* symbols, catching up in their compactness a wide variety of possible meanings that can, subsequently, be differentiated out, given greater or lesser emphasis, or even eliminated. A political society dedicated to the glorification of God and the advancement of the faith might, for example, easily convince itself that it must become a *theocracy*, a society ruled by saints; it might decide that because it is dedicated to God it has been chosen by God, is in some meaningful sense God's own society;

it might understand the obligation to advance the faith as authorizing it to spread the faith by the sword, and to slaughter any infidels that stand in its way; it might decide that it can glorify God and advance the faith only by building the Promised Land, which, in turn, it might decide to be a matter of building it here on earth, or a matter of building it in the world to come. The possibilities, we can readily see, are numerous, and the symbolization is compact in the sense that it nails none of them down; it leaves to the future, rather, all the decisions as to what, concretely, the symbols mean, what, concretely, they involve in the way of specific commitments.[3]

Second: The same is true with respect to the symbols "due Submission and Obedience," "just and equal Laws," laws "thought [to be] most meet and convenient for the general Good." They also catch up in their compactness an infinite variety of potential developments. The symbol "just and equal Laws" might be emphasized, off in the future, at the expense of the symbol "laws . . . *thought* [to be] most meet and convenient for the general Good" [4]—in which case the society might move in the direction of a new symbol, a government of laws and not of men. Or the *"thought* to be" might be emphasized at the expense of the "just and equal," or the "due obedience," in which case we would have, off at the end, the absolute sovereignty of public opinion—the insistence on the identity between what people *think* to be just and equal laws and justice. Or, again, the *"thought* to be" might be emphasized, and the political society might, for instance, adopt as its central problem the elaboration of procedures for thinking laws through completely before they are adopted— in which case what we have termed above *deliberation* might

---

[3] We shall see that the Constitution does nail down the specific commitments once and for all. See our subsequent discussion.
[4] Emphasis added.

separate off as the supreme symbol, yet with the society remaining within the confines, verbal and spiritual, of the original symbolism.

Third: the signers say nothing, *unless by implication*, about their *individual rights*. Similarly, except in the phrase "just and equal Laws," they have nothing to say about equality. We should pause and think very hard about that because it might seem to suggest that—since we hear often that freedom and equality are the supreme symbols of American political society—the Mayflower Compact cannot possibly be the beginning, the act of founding of American political society. First, we must be absolutely clear about what we mean when we say that the Compact says nothing explicit about rights but may say something by *implication* about them. This is to say—and the point is of critical importance for what follows—that one might start out from the Compact and arrive at some rights by some such logic as the following: The signers owe not obedience but only *due* obedience, and not to all laws but only to such just and equal laws as are thought to contribute to the general good. Take that a step further, and it would seem to follow logically that the signers recognize an obligation, or *duty*, to govern by just and equal laws deemed necessary for the public good. Take that another step further, and it would seem to follow that each signer has henceforth an individual right to the performance of that duty by his fellow-signers; as, too, it would seem to follow that tomorrow, when the just and equal laws go into effect, he will find himself the proud owner or enjoyer of some rights that will be conferred by those just and equal laws. One might say, then, that the Compact does perhaps imply some individual rights, that is, at second remove, though we do not learn from the language of the Compact just what those rights are. One might say that that is precisely what the deliberations—tomorrow's and tomorrow's and tomorrow's—will be about; that is what, in the language of the Compact, new determinations will be made about "from time to time." One might even say that yes, the Compact confers some rights, but of a highly *general* character and in any case of a *derivative* character—a right to justice, and a right to the performance, by each signer's fellow-signers, of the duties to be imposed by the laws thought to be conducive to the general good. To use currently fashionable language, the supreme "values" of the system—for, yes, we begin to see it is a system we have before us—are *justice* and *general good*. Rights, we can well imagine, will emerge from future discussions of justice and the general good, and will be embodied in laws representing a *consensus* about justice and the general good; so that (*a*) the Compact recognizably lays down, so to speak, a program for future political discussions in the colony (they are, however, to concern themselves in the first instance with justice and the general good, not individual rights) and (*b*) the authors of the Compact can say all that they need to say without mentioning individual rights. And we begin to see, it would appear, why the Framers of the Philadelphia Constitution, insofar as they were faithful heirs of the symbolization of the Mayflower Compact, fought shy of any attempt to make a list of individual rights—and why the Preamble to the Constitution, in reciting the purposes of the Constitution is to serve, does not so much as mention individual rights, but does, as we should expect since it was written by heirs of the Compact, place justice and the general welfare, that is, the general good, among the highest goods of the emergent Union. But more about this later.

So too with equality: Equality, that is equality in any meaning of the term that would be acceptable to the custodians of our official literature, is wholly absent from the vocabulary of the authors of the Compact. The colony, to be sure, is to have just and equal laws, but there is no suggestion that just laws are laws that—to come right to the major issues in this area—

treat all persons equally, or tend to promote equality among all persons. There is no suggestion, either, that all the persons concerned are to have an equal voice in the enacting of those laws or—a point of similar importance—that all persons are *not* to have an equal voice in the making of those laws. And the Philadelphia Constitution again comes to mind: equality is not among the goods to which it commits us in its Preamble. Indeed the suspicion arises—now is as good a time as any to get it into words—that those who tell us that freedom and equality, with freedom understood as a matter of individual rights, are the supreme symbols of the American political tradition, might well be talking through their hats or really mean to say that somewhere along the line, somewhere after the Compact and the Constitution, the tradition somehow turned itself upside down.

Fourth: Let us notice, for what it is worth, that the Compact breathes above all the spirit of *moderation*. The glorification of God and the advancement of the faith, though indeed present as symbols, figure in the Compact as obligations, commitments, that the signers presumably share with other believers in God, other participants in faith. There is no suggestion that they think of themselves as peculiarly *chosen* for the purposes named (we are, remember, dealing with a variant of the Moses myth) as in any special sense God's people —if sentiments of that kind are in due course to be heard in America (as they were heard in due course), they will come as *departures* from the Compact symbolization. More: The signers, as we come to know them through the Compact, appear to be making no extravagant claims for themselves even in connection with their determination to give themselves just and equal laws conducive to the general good. This is the real significance of their injecting "thought most meet and convenient for the general Good," wherein the implication is that the problem of doing justice and defining and promoting the general good is an extremely difficult problem, for the solution of which they lay claim to no inside track, no special gift beyond the disposition to have a go at it, to think together, to think carefully, and arrive at agreed conclusions. There is no other implication, therefore, that they are about to usher in a new world order, that with them history is taking its great turning point, that they will bring into being a new breed of men that will put to shame all humankind as it has been known in the past. The signers state themselves, rather, in terms of traditional political thought, the political thought of the preceding centuries (the glorification of God, the advancement of the faith, justice, the common good) , and think of themselves as continuing a task already begun, even already carried to high levels of achievement, in the past. And wherever and whenever men in America have spoken the language of moderation and evinced piety toward the past, we may fairly speak of them as heirs of the Mayflower Compact.

Fifth: The Compact tells us nothing about *how* laws are to be enacted or who is to govern in the body politic that is being founded. It is almost as if the signers were blissfully unaware of what we fashionably call the problem of political power. One might even say that they seem not to know, not yet, how free they are because they do not yet know what shape their freedom will take on tomorrow—in the course of that tomorrow when they will discover that they must, like it or not, govern *themselves*. All of which is to say (and we deliberately use the language of the Preamble of the Constitution) , they will have to provide for the common defense, insure domestic tranquility, form a more perfect Union, and yet, somehow, still secure the blessings of liberty to themselves and their posterity. All of that, tomorrow, will become *the* problem, as, in America, it has been *the* problem ever since, has had to be *the* problem in America as it had never been anywhere or at any time because once in America they simply had to govern themselves because there was no one else to do the job for them. The signers do not know it, but in the Compact they have merely established a society, not a government, so that their symbols, with the passing of time, will have to be revised in order to provide for the relationship between society and government, between the social order and the specifically political order.

Finally: The Compact, as we have noted, says nothing about rights, nothing about equality. But let that not blind us to one obvious fact, namely: The Compact is itself an exercise in freedom, and a tacit assertion of at least one right, that is, the right to be free, the right to make such a compact as the signers are making. Similarly, the Compact does assert a certain kind of equality, namely, an equal capacity on the part of the signers to give or withhold consent.[5] We might fairly expect, then, that if in due course the Compact itself becomes a symbol of a new society, that society will assert that kind of freedom and that kind of equality and will, therefore, place a high value on getting everybody's consent to its law, or, at least, on achieving consensus.

[5] This right of consent, as we shall maintain, is the only meaningful "right" asserted in the Declaration of Independence.

CHAPTER III

Political Order:
The Connecticut and
Massachusetts Experiences

We can for good reason deal more briefly with the pre-Declaration of Independence documents on our list because we already have the main elements of the problem in hand. That is, more precisely, we know the main things we must look for in order to decide whether there is continuity from the Mayflower Compact to the Declaration of Independence and the Constitution. We will look first at the Fundamental Orders of Connecticut,[1] composed nineteen years after the Mayflower Compact, and ask this question: Are we, in the Fundamental Orders, still dealing with the Mayflower symbols, albeit in a more or less differentiated form? The answer, we think, is Yes. The Fundamental Orders, like our Mayflower document, are recognizably a *compact,* to which, presumably, all agree, to which all, symbolically at least, are signers. "We," the document reads, "do . . . associate and conjoin ourselves to be as one Public State or Commonwealth: and . . . do enter into Combination and Confederation together . . . ." The "civil body politic" of the Mayflower Compact, however, has become a "public state or commonwealth," and—a not insignificant matter, we think—the word "convenant" has disappeared from the formulation, which suggests, as we have previously noted, that the Mayflower Compact has become a symbol so familiar and meaningful that

---

[1] Poore, I, 249–51. We have modernized the spelling.

it is capable of merely tacit evocation. Put otherwise: The fact of convenanting, of making an oath, or requiring an oath from one another, is already taken as a matter of course; the signers, at this stage, have only to fill in the terms, without bothering to mention that the terms add up to a convenant (as the May-flower signers did not have to mention that they were reen-acting the convenant at Mt. Sinai). Now, however, it is not a "civil body politic," but a "public state or commonwealth," which may or may not be significant—though it does suggest that the specifically political order, the problem of power, of government, has been differentiated out, separated off, from that of the social order. And there are two new purposes, exactly the two, furthermore, that we missed from the May-flower Compact when we were comparing it with the Pream-ble of the Philadelphia Constitution, as we see from the words: "to maintain the peace" (the Philadelphia Constitution will say "to insure domestic Tranquility") and to maintain "union" (the Philadelphia Constitution will say "to form a more perfect union"). We have, therefore, two new symbols, the need for which did not occur to the Mayflower signers, who as we have pointed out had not yet grasped some of the exigencies of their new situation. (Still missing, among the purposes of the Philadelphia Preamble we might notice in passing, are: "to provide for the common defence" and "to secure the Blessings of Liberty.") Note also that the glorifica-tion of God" and the "advancement of the faith" seem to have disappeared—though we have in their place (ominously, some might say) a differentiated symbol which, however, the Connecticut signers would claim catches up and improves the meaning of the missing Mayflower symbols. What we have now is: "to maintain and preserve the liberty and purity of the gospel of our Lord Jesus which we now profess, as also the discipline of the Churches, which according to the truth of said gospel is now practiced amongst us." If, then, we have moved towards differentiation of the political order, we have also lumped into it the religious order; the public commonwealth or state has as one of its tasks that of maintaining, of course, the purity of the gospel and the discipline of the churches. That is not to say that the folk on the Mayflower had in their hearts a different intention. But it is to say that the intention to assimilate the political and religious order in this way had not yet entered into their understanding of themselves, and therefore could not be articulated—although, surprisingly, perhaps, the Mayflower Compact becomes, in this regard, continuous with the Philadelphia Constitution in a way in which the Connecticut Orders cannot, since the Constitution will dispel any possible confusion between the political order and religion.

What else do we find? Consonant with what has been said, and reminiscent of another point made toward the end of the second chapter, we note the following wholly new emphasis: The "we" of the Connecticut Fundamental Orders identify themselves as "we the inhabitants" of such and such towns, and, further, as we who "are now cohabiting and dwelling" in such and such a place. Now this emphasis is highly important for a reason that the Mayflower Covenanters do not mention, namely: "It hath pleased the Almighty God by the wise disposition of His divine providence so to order and dispose of things." This literally interpreted does begin to sound a little like a claim to be in some special sense God's people, and helps explain the concern for the discipline of the churches as "now practiced amongst us"—which may or may not involve a claim to a special relationship with God, a relationship that peoples who inhabit other places do not have. And still another new emphasis: The task of "better ordering" of the Mayflower Compact now becomes, in the first instance, the more differentiated task of bringing into being an "orderly and decent government," a further solid Connecticut contribution

to our basic symbols (which do indeed include the maintenance of an orderly and decent government) but with two
(again perhaps ominus) further twists; the government is
to be a government "established according to God" and a
government that will maintain peace and union *because* "the
word of God requires" maintenance of a government for these
purposes. (Both of these further twists will be dropped at
Philadelphia, but were perhaps more or less still present in
the five states that, in 1789, still had established religions. But
from the standpoint of the later development, Connecticut
here offers us an example of what Voegelin would call a "de-
railing" of the original symbolization, and, at the same time,
let us note, a move away from the language and spirit of
moderation.)

The best example of differentiation that occurs between
the Compact and the Fundamental Orders, as we should
expect and have already begun to notice, is the further specification of the already differentiated symbol of "orderly and
decent government." That government, we learn, is "to order
and dispose of the affairs of the people at all seasons as occasion shall require" and it is to be "guided and governed
according to . . . Laws, Rules, Orders, and decrees . . . ," which
brings us very close to the workings of the American government in even recent times. And the most important step of
all, perhaps, because it gives us our first example of a constitution, that is, a written statement of the procedures by which
laws are to be made and enforced, and so a new highly differentiated symbol that is to become the central problem for
critical clarification in America: "Laws, Rules, Orders and
decrees . . . shall be made, ordered, and decreed, as *followeth*."
And still another, also destined to be a central preoccupation
of American political discourse is the representative assembly
—or, as it is called in Connecticut, the general assembly, about
which we learn the following: The inhabitants of each town

—that is, specifically, all who have taken the oath of fidelity—
are at specified intervals to "meet and assemble together" to
elect and choose their deputies to the general assembly (each
deputy to be himself a freeman of the commonwealth of Connecticut). The general assembly is to meet twice yearly, once
as a court of election that will name "seven magistrates and
other public officers" (one of the magistrates will be named to
serve as governor for one year; the other six will be empowered to "administer justice according to the law here established"—or, where there is no applicable law, "according to
the rule of the word of God"). No magistrate is to be chosen
for more than one year; the magistrates shall be sworn according to an oath; elections shall be by majority vote of those
present, as, on the local level, individuals are to become inhabitants, and thus eligible to vote for the deputies, by *majority
vote* of the inhabitants. No one shall serve as governor more
than once in any two-year period, and in order to serve as
governor a man must previously have served as magistrate and
must be a member of some approved religious congregation
(and we may note again the continued lumping into the
political order of religious considerations). As for the general
court, in it shall reside "the supreme power of the Commonwealth." It alone shall make or repeal laws, grant levies, and
dispose of undisposed lands; it shall, besides, have the power to
"call into question," for any misdemeanor, any magistrate or
any other person whatever, and to deal with the culprit "according to the nature of the offence" (it may, for example,
remove the offending magistrate from office). And the general
assembly may, finally, "deal in any other matter that concerns
the good of this commonwealth." A quorum for a general
assembly, we notice (the Orders do not use the word quorum,
but the idea is there), shall consist of the governor or a moder-
ator elected *ad hoc*, at least four magistrates, and a majority of
the deputies chosen by the towns. And the governor or mod-

erator shall have the power "to give liberty of speech," that is, to recognize speakers, to silence "unseasonable and disorderly speakings," to put matters to vote, and himself to vote in the case of a tie. And a general assembly may be adjourned only by a majority vote of the participants.

All of this, we should recall, is set forth only nineteen years after the Mayflower Compact. Yet two of the Compact symbols, the "better ordering" and the "enact, constitute, and frame . . . just and equal laws" have become, by what Voegelin calls differentiation, a cluster of new symbols that are to be the very stuff of subsequent American politics: the written constitution; the supremacy of what is recognizably a legislature, though still an undifferentiated legislature from which the executive and judiciary, though themselves present in recognizable form, have not yet separated off; majority votes, both for elections and for the passing of laws. The basic symbols, in a word, are moving rapidly in the direction of the symbolization of the years 1776–89, when the American political system as we know it will have taken pretty much final shape. But let us hasten on to Massachusetts and Virginia, pausing only to note the following:

First: There is still no differentiation of the Mayflower symbols in the direction of individual rights. To put this otherwise, on the level that we associate with individual rights, we hear in Connecticut only of the "supreme power of the commonwealth" as residing in the general assembly. The laws of the commonwealth, that is, the duties the commonwealth imposes and the rights it guarantees, are those decided upon at a meeting of elected representatives from the several towns, acting by majority vote, ordering and disposing of the affairs of the people at all seasons as occasion shall require. Indeed, the "thought to be meet and convenient," which as we know is one symobolic standard for law-making laid down in the Compact, appears now to have been emphasized at the expense

of all else. Within this newly differentiated political order
there is nothing to compete with the "thought to be meet and
convenient," that is, the judgment of the legislature. A man's
rights, it is hardly too much to say, are simply those the general
assembly chooses to give him.

Second: What we miss above all in the differentiated
Connecticut symbols is the "just and equal laws" symbol of
the Mayflower Compact, and we must keep our eyes open for
its next appearance on the scene. For that symbol, alone among
the Mayflower symbols, holds compactly within it the promise
of the symbol of a *higher law,* not necessarily that of the Bible,
which can be used as a standard by which to judge and eval-
uate the determination of mere law-making authorities.

We move now to Massachusetts and to a time (1641) two
years later than that of the Connecticut Fundamental Orders.

The Massachusetts Body of Liberties[2] describes itself as a
"further establishing of this Government"—that is, as a
rounding-out of a constitution already in existence. And it
gives us at once a new symbol, namely, that of the "liberties,
immunities and privileges . . . due to every man"—or, as it calls
them a moment later, "freedoms," which does indeed begin
to sound like individual rights. Certain freedoms, it affirms,
are called for by "humanity, civility [the "civil body politic"
of the Mayflower Compact], and Christianity." The "free fru-
ition" which we may take to mean the continued expansion of
these liberties or freedoms "hath ever been and ever will be
the tranquility and stability of Churches and Commonwealth," just as their "denial or deprival" brings both "disturbance" and "ruin" to both Church and Commonwealth.
Now, The Framers' purpose is nothing less than to get down in
black and white "all such freedoms as for [the] present we

---

[2] Our quotes are taken from the *Colonial Laws of Massachusetts* (Compiled
by Order of the City Council of Boston under the direction of Mr. S. Whitmore,
1889) . We have modernized the spelling.

foresee may concern us, and our posterity after us"; to "decree and confirm" those freedoms "to be respectively, impartially, and inviolably enjoyed and observed throughout our jurisdiction forever." They ratified these freedoms with their solemn consent, "religiously and unanimously." Apparently, at least, we stand in the presence, for America at least, of the first attempt at a Bill or Declaration of Rights; and it is this aspect of the matter that deserves our attention.

Let us take as our point of departure this question: Are the good folk of Massachusetts, as we see them interpreting themselves here, interpreting themselves as servants of "humanity, Civility, and Christianity," are they indeed understanding themselves as possessed of what we today call rights—and, if so, are these "rights" the "rights of Englishmen?" This is, we believe, a good question, and will lead us to some surprises for though the rhetoric indeed anticipates the day (it will come at the conclusion of the Philadelphia Convention) when some Americans will wish to set down in black and white those rights of every man that government must not invade, we shall find that the business here in hand is very far from that indeed. And this for the following reasons:

(1) We have deliberately omitted one phrase from our discussion of the Massachusetts document that is of decisive importance. The freedoms they are about to set down are "due" to "every man," *but* the document continues, "due to every *man in his place and proportion.*" [3] Whatever we stand in the presence of, therefore, it is not the symbol of equal rights. The point is, rather, that the freedoms differ from man to man, and belong to each man to a degree or proportion that depends on the place he occupies. The words "due" and "proportion," one might say, put us on warning that the folk of Massachusetts are concerned not about equality, but about *justice* as it has been understood traditionally (thus the strik-

3 Emphasis added.

ing reference to humanity, civility, and Christianity, and to that which has *"ever* been," that is, traditionally been, the tranquility and stability of churches and commonwealths).

(2) The liberties or rights listed do indeed, at least some of them, have a familiar sound for our ears and would not at first glance seem to be out of place in a modern Bill of Rights. Paragraph 1 of the document appears, for instance, to assert the very right, or complex of rights, that we find at the beginning of the Declaration of Independence, and find more or less echoed in the Fifth Amendment of Madison's Bill of Rights. It appears, that is, to assert an individual right to "life, liberty, and the pursuit of happiness." Similarly, paragraph 43 appears to be a guarantee against cruel and unusual punishment; 42 a guarantee against what we today call double jeopardy; 6 a guarantee against involuntary servitude; and 18 seems to be a guarantee of habeas corpus—all of which is reminiscent of contemporary constitutional law. *But*—and this brings us to a very crucial point—we readily see that the guarantees (like those of our present Bill of Rights) fall into two categories:[4] (*a*) those that guarantee this or that immunity against violation by a court of law, or an executive official, and (*b*) those that, if they were going to mean what we say we mean by rights today, would have to guarantee against the legislative authority, or, as it is called here, the General

---

[4] The document itself draws this very distinction. It is divided into major sections, one of which is, to quote literally, the "Rites Rules and Liberties concerning Juditiall proceedings." Other sections include: "Liberties of Woemen," "Liberties of Children," "Liberties of Servants," and "Liberties of Forreiners and Strangers." All of this would certainly suggest that the drafters viewed the matter of parcelling out liberties and rights from a different perspective than our contemporary intellectuals.

What would be more shocking to those who presume to know the American tradition are the following passages (and again we use the literal language) : "If any man after legall conviction shall have or worship any other god, but the lord god, he shall be put to death." "If any man or woman be a witch (that is hath or consulteth with a familiar spirit,) They shall be put to death." These provisions fall under the category of "Capitall Laws."

On these and like matters see our discussion below.

Court. There are several instances of category (a); no man can be put to death "without the testimony of two or three witnessess"; "no man shall be beaten with above 40 stripes," and no "true gentleman" (note here the distinction between "man" and "gentleman") shall be whipped at all "unless his crime be very shameful, etc."; no man shall be forced by tortures to confess to any crime except in capital cases where he has been fully convicted, although then, if there be a suspicion that he has had confederates, he may be tortured, though not in a barbarous or inhumane manner. To say the least, these are not very comforting guarantees or rights. But the point here is that they are, in any case, guarantees against the judges and executive officials, and *not* guarantees against the legislature. As for category (b), rights that we might expect to be guaranteed against legislative encroachment or violation—and this we must take great care to note—contain escape clauses. Each of the relevant guarantees is, so to speak, a verbal parachute that from the standpoint of the official literature would reduce it to meaninglessness. Allow us to illustrate this:

Paragraph 1 says in effect: No man shall be deprived of life, liberty, property, or the pursuit of happiness unless by virtue of some express law established by the General Court! Paragraph 5 says in effect that no man shall be pressed into involuntary labor unless it be "grounded upon some act of the General Court"! Paragraph 18 says that no man shall be imprisoned before being sentenced by law, or denied liberty on bail, except in capital crimes, etc., unless "some express act of the [General] Court shall allow it." What the Body of Liberties of Massachusetts does, then, as regards our category (b) is to identify certain areas that we might fairly call sensitive from the standpoint of freedom, reserve them to the colony's deliberative assembly, and to assert that in those areas a man's rights are those that the legislature decided to vouchsafe to him. There is no hint, we see now, of any right *against* the legislature, of any liberty or immunity that the legislature *must* vouchsafe to each man, because he is a man. Moreover, there is no hint of any right that *limits* the power of the legislature. One might well say that the "better ordering" and the "thought-to-be-meet-and-convenient-for-the general-Good" symbols of the Mayflower Compact have differentiated out into the symbol of an omnicompetent and legally omnipotent deliberative assembly. And this, at first blush, appears to be the supreme symbol for the political order (which of course still embraces both Church and State). Both "justice" and the "general Good" seem to have disappeared as symbols, or, to put it the other way around, the good folk of Massachusetts seem to have repudiated justice and the general good as standards for their body politic and, to that extent, to have moved out of the basic symbolization of the Mayflower Compact. And the question arises—can, indeed, no longer be postponed—What are we to make of this? Are the good folk of Massachusetts setting themselves up as their *own* standard, or as being capable, in and of themselves, of serving as a source of standards? Is all the talk in the Body of Liberties about freedoms, immunities, etc., just talk?

Let us take up this question in easy stages.

(1) The Body of Liberties is put forward as reflecting a unanimous *consent*. It is a reenactment of the *rite* involved in the symbol for the Mayflower Compact, which as we have seen did emphasize the absence of any dissident or any dissident group. But in dealing with the Compact, we did not ask, as now we must, *Why* all the insistence on unanimous consent? *Why* continue the deliberation, why go on deliberating, until all are ready to sign? *Why* make of the unanimous signers one of the supreme symbols? One obvious answer—and one that perpetuates itself down through American history with respect to the loyalty oath—is that the oathtakers are engaged in what

they deem an important enterprise, and want, therefore, to know what kind of people they are dealing with. In other words, the enterprise, which in the original symbolization is a civil body politic dedicated to the glorification of God and the advancement of the faith, is not the kind of enterprise on which you launch yourself with just anybody, not the kind of enterprise you go into except with people in whom you have *confidence*. The individuals in the saloon of the Mayflower may, to be sure, be presumed to have known right smart about each other, but at the last minute that seems to be not enough: They want to nail down their important common beliefs, want each man to stand up and be counted as one who in fact believes these things, want to be in a position to say to any man who acts as if he did *not* believe these things: "See here, you have committed yourself on this; you must not go back on your commitment." Knowing, each of them, what the others believe, they know or think they know what they can expect of each other in the way of conduct (beliefs, we would say in contemporary social science jargon, are "predictive" of "behavior"). The people, in the moment of constituting and interpreting itself as a people, does so in terms of the individual beliefs of the persons coming together. The people, one might say, is what the people believes, knows itself to believe, and can be counted upon to act on.

Massachusetts, as we have intimated, simply reenacts the Mayflower Compact *rite* and, similarly, it writes into the Body of Liberties the equivalent of a *creed* which will presumably govern its future deliberations—not, to be sure, the same creed as the Mayflower Creed, but recognizably the Mayflower Creed as differentiated in the course of further political experience, some of it, no doubt, the political experience of nearby Connecticut (which also left out justice, or rather simply equated it with the gospel). Now, we cannot attend too carefully to the Massachusetts specification: One of the high symbols it evokes is, as we have seen, humanity, civility, and Christianity, which, we are told, "call for" certain things, which the Body of Liberties is about to perform. The people of Massachusetts understand themselves, then, as servants of humanity, civility, and Christianity, as called upon to do that which is humane, civil, and Christian. They unanimously signify that they are *servants* of humanity, civility, and Christianity, and as such servants, accept their call of humanity, civility, and Christianity. And the breath-taking powers attributed to the General Court must be understood in that context: The General Court that is to pass laws on the delicate topics touched upon, to pass laws in the sensitive areas from the standpoint of freedom, is to be made up of servants of humanity, civility and Christianity, sitting as a deliberative body, and subordinate to the "call" of humanity, civility, and Christianity. There is no implication, no hint of a suggestion, that humanity, civility, and Christianity are, from the standpoint of the General Court, other than given, no hint of a suggestion that the General Court is entitled to improvise when dealing with the question: What is humane? and civil? and Christian? The gospel of the Connecticut Orders, one might say, has broadened to include humanity and civility, which words we do not overtax when we summarize them as philosophy, as the great tradition of Western man's thought about the humane and civil. The appeal, then, is to the transcendent truth of the soul and society as continuously explored by Western man, over the centuries, through the experience of philosophy and religion. And Massachusetts, differentiating out some of the potentialities of the Mayflower Compact symbols, gives us one of the lasting symbols of the American political experience, namely, that of deliberation on the affairs of the people, on, that is, the general good, in an atmosphere in which arguments may be drawn, indifferently, from the philosophic and religious tradition of the West. We must not be surprised, then, when we re-read *The Federalist,* to find that that is precisely the Federalist's understanding of deliberation. Or— to put the whole point a little differently, and to come to one of the central tensions or paradoxes of the American political experience—we find implicit in the Mayflower Compact symbol, specified now in Massachusetts, the potential symbol of the virtuous people, the people who understands itself as virtuous because subordinated to the transcendent truth of the soul and of society, and because it has demanded of the persons who are its individual components that by "signing" they signify their subordination, as persons, to that truth. That is why the Mayflower Compact can exact submission to laws *thought* to be meet and convenient for the general good; and that is why Massachusetts can equate the "liberties, immunities and privileges" called for by humanity, civility, and Christianity with the determinations of its General Court, and deem it unnecessary to make further provision for them. The apparent conflict between the symbol of a higher law, compounded of humanity, civility, and Christianity, on the one hand, and the symbol of a supreme legislature that is the immediate source of legal rights and duties that cannot be stipulated beforehand is, we are saying, resolved by the further symbol of the virtuous people. And this symbol will be the object of subsequent critical clarification so that we should not be surprised to find this symbol hauled out into the open by Publius to resolve the central problem he has set for himself.

But to other points:

The symbols *higher law, supreme representative assembly, deliberation,* the *virtuous people,* are to take their places among the constants of America's self-interpretation. Let us briefly fix our attention on the second of these symbols, which we saw emerge (as far as our documents are concerned) with the Connecticut General Orders. The people, even *if* virtuous, cannot deliberate, or at least cannot once the people has ceased to be a small group gathered in the saloon of the Mayflower, and cannot, in any case, once the problems are sufficiently complex and difficult to require a certain level of intellectual achievement. The people must, then, deliberate through representatives, and that calls, to go no further, for machinery through which representatives are chosen, as also, a point on which Massachusetts is explicit, for *confederation* issues (think how predictive that is of the later American experience, which now has us confederating even with Hawaii!). Now, if that machinery is good machinery, it will channel the virtue of the virtuous people, their subordination to a higher law, into the decisions arrived at, through deliberation, by the virtuous people's representatives. On the other hand, if the machinery be bad, it may fail to channel the people's virtue into those decisions, in which case legal rights and duties will not correspond to the call of humanity, civility, and Christianity. It is not too much to say that the goodness or badness of the representative machinery turns, clearly, on whether it does channel the virtue of the people into the decisions concerning legal rights and duties; and we recognize at once the possibility of differentiating out the symbol of the representative assembly, the assembly that truly represents the virtue of the people, as a topic for critical clarification. And again we must not be surprised, when we re-read *The Federalist*, to see *that* problem hauled out into the open as a central problem for the American symbolization.

Secondly, although alike in Connecticut and Massachusetts (nor shall we find it different in Virginia), one part of the Mayflower Compact seems to have disappeared completely; we hear no more (curiously, considering the date) of His Majesty the King of Great Britain, or of the honour of the king and of Great Britain, as one of the purposes to be served by the civil body politic. The problem that the Mayflower covenanters did not face back there in the ship's saloon, and that we said they *must* face the next day, the problem of governing themselves, governing themselves necessarily, because loyal subjects of the king though they be, the king and his ministers are not *there* to govern them—that problem, clearly, has now monopolized the minds of the heirs of the Mayflower Compact. One might say that the Mayflower Compact was composed, as we can see it in retrospect, by a people far more free than it understands itself to be; and that the General Orders and the Body of Liberties are composed by a people who already have the habit of freedom and the habit of self-government—and this despite the fact they may still think of themselves, tacitly, as subjects of the king. When, therefore, they put into words the liberties, immunities, etc., that they understand themselves as entitled to, we notice now, what they lay claim to is, so to speak, the rights of being governed by their own representatives, the rights of self-government. We must keep that in mind: When our ancestors in Massachusetts spoke of the rights, their "liberties, immunities, and privileges" that they ought to have, they appear to have meant something quite different, something prior to, than what many of our contemporaries mean when they speak of "rights." Our ancestors meant self-government, that is, democracy, which we now know to have been in the process of being born between the Mayflower Compact and the Constitution.

Third, and finally, with the symbols we have in hand we must ask: What is to keep the virtuous people virtuous? The question is as old as Greek philosophy, and Greek philosophy offered, on one level at least, the decisive answer: The people will be virtuous only to the extent that the souls of its individual components are rightly ordered, and the right ordering of souls is the business of education. That would call, in the language of the Massachusetts Body of Liberties, for education capable of ordering individual souls in accordance with the principles of humanity, civility, and Christianity; and education appropriate to the maintenance of the virtue of the people cries up at us as a further problem that wants critical clarification. One might, indeed, argue that failure to meet this problem head on has been perhaps the greatest failure of the American political experience, and we are entitled to be surprised when we find that Publius seems to be unaware of education as a problem for the new republic.

What we have said to this point is sufficient to bring into focus the central paradox or tension which we may formulate as follows: American political society expresses itself, from an early moment, in the symbol of the supreme legislature on the one hand, and on the other of a higher law that the supreme legislature must apply to day-to-day problems. It does not express itself in terms of individual rights; or at least not in terms of individual rights against the legislature, individual rights that the legislature must respect, must not violate. Individual rights may subsequently become—we are often told today that they have become—the essence of the American political tradition, but if so, we may confidently say here in Massachusetts, that that will be a later development and, we may now add, a development hard to fit into the Mayflower-Connecticut-Massachusetts symbolism.

Let us explore briefly why this is so. The issue in question is *not* whether individuals *have* rights. Of course individuals have rights, and so far as we know no one has ever questioned that. *The* primary issue with respect to this matter is what do you talk about first. Do you talk first about the individual and the rights that he ought to have, ought to enjoy, or do you talk first about some other things, and most particularly one other thing, namely: the general good? It would seem that most Americans thought until recently that you talk first about the general or common good, because the rights that individuals ought to have are, neither more nor less, those required, those called for, by the common good; that, therefore, the vocabulary of individual rights is not a good vocabulary with which to discuss the problems of politics. Still another issue of critical importance can be put as follows: Who is to *say*, at any given moment and whatever the case may be concerning individual rights, what rights on the part of individuals are to be made legal rights? Is someone going to list them beforehand, and say to the legislature: This is it, boys—or is that precisely what the legislature is there to deliberate and legislate about according to its best lights? Translated into language of the contemporary scene, that becomes the question: Who is to say whom Mrs. Murphy is to admit as roomers in her boarding house, that is, whether everybody has a right to stay at Mrs. Murphy's, whether Mrs. Murphy has a right to exclude from her rooming house people she does not wish to accommodate. Now, down to a very recent moment, as we shall see more fully later, the American answer to that question was quite simply: Not a Supreme Court, not a Chief Executive, not, most particularly, some minority parading placards through the streets, but a representative assembly that We the People elect, and elect precisely to make that kind of decision for us, and in the course of its deliberations, reenactments always of the deliberation there in the saloon of the Mayflower, about the general good.

There are, of course, other possible answers to that question. The vast corpus of literature, for example, which downgrades Congress and the state legislatures is full of other possible answers. But the answer provided for us at a very early stage in the American tradition is that our deliberative assemblies should make such determinations.

CHAPTER IV

Rights and the Virginia Declaration

We come, at last, to a moment close to the beginning of the American political tradition as, that is, the official literature understands it. The date is June 12, 1776, only a few weeks before the Declaration of Independence. From the Massachusetts Body of Liberties, that is to say, we take a jump of nearly a century and a half—time enough, in all conscience, for quite a change in people's self-interpretation, unless, of course, it has found itself content, more or less, with the self-interpretation it started out with. *One* thing has changed, certainly, and that is the rhetoric: The document before us, commonly referred to as the Virginia Bill of Rights (technically the Virginia Declaration of Rights) ,[1] contains a word that we have not run across before in the documents we have been examining, and we are obliged therefore to ask: Does the sudden shift to the vocabulary of "rights" involve a shift, a genuine change, in the self-interpretation of the American political society? Does "rights," as the word is used by the "representatives of the good people of Virginia, assembled in full and free convention," bring us close to the sort of thing the proponents of the Bill of Rights *are said*, thirteen years later, to have in mind?

Our first impression is that "yes," a shift has occurred, and there *is*, indeed, something new under the political sun. The rights in question, we are told early in the Virginia Declara-

[1] Poore, II, 1908–909.

tion, are *inherent* rights of all men (this does sound very much
like the Declaration of Independence, and the American "tradition" of natural rights as glorified by the official literature) .
"All men," it says, "have certain *inherent* rights," and those
rights because all men are "by nature" (another word we have
not been hearing before) *"free and independent."* [2] More still:
An *inherent right* turns out to be a right that belongs to each
man so much as a matter of course, so much as a part or aspect
of his being a man, that he himself cannot, we are told, can-
not, upon entering a state of society, renounce it for his posterity (nor, we may infer though the document does not say so,
for himself) , not even by his own consent, not even by compact.[3] But let us explore these and related matters at some
length.

   Two things, we may remind ourselves, had happened in the
English-speaking world between the Massachusetts Body of
Liberties and the Virginia Declaration of Rights that might
help account for the shift, if one has occurred, in our self-
understanding during this period. First: In 1689 the British
Parliament had adopted or, more accurately, forced on their
king, a Bill of Rights, which had as its primary purpose the
imposition of certain limitations upon the power of the king.
Second, and probably more important in light of contemporary intellectual interpretations of our tradition, John
Locke had published, hard on the heels of the English Bill of
Rights, a book that set forth the idea that man once lived in a
state of nature, that is, had once lived without law or government; and that in this state of nature, there had held sway a
law of nature, the essence of which is that man in the state of

   2 Emphasis added.
   3 The text reads as follows: "That all men are by nature equally free and
independent, and have certain inherent rights, of which, when they enter into
a state of society, they cannot, by any compact, deprive or divest their posterity;
namely, the enjoyment of life and liberty, with the means of acquiring and
possessing property, and pursuing and obtaining happiness and safety."

nature is born with a right, his *by* nature, to self-preservation; that man had emerged from the state of nature and entered into society by virtue of a freely negotiated compact, by which, so to speak, he trades off his natural right to self-preservation (making sure, of course, that he gets a good deal) in return for the privilege of living under government that is *limited* in the sense that there are certain things which he (man) specifies beforehand, that it is not empowered to do. Those things which government should not do yield up his *rights*, which are precisely rights he holds *against* government, that government must not violate.

Now, according to our official literature, America had, in the course of the eighteenth century, come under the influence of Locke—as we see at once, so exponents of the official literature would tell us, from the Virginians' use of the term "by nature," of the term "inherent rights," of the term "enter into a state of society," and of the term "compact." We concede at once this much: *If* the Americans did indeed become Lockeans in the course of the decades preceding 1776, then there did indeed occur a shift in self-understanding, *not* a mere shift in rhetoric. We concede at once, too, that we cannot prove that the Virginians to whom we are now listening had not fallen under Locke's spell—which is, let us emphasize, a potent spell, capable of producing strange behavior on a scale that would put to shame the spell of a mere Svengali. While we cannot prove that the Virginians were not Lockeans, we *can* say, and say with profound conviction, that the charge cannot be proved out of the document before us. The term "compact," as we know, entered the vocabulary of American politics more than half a century before Locke even published his wonder-working book; "rights," as used by the Virginians, may well refer only to the kind of thing the folk of Massachusetts had in mind when they spoke of their "liberties"; the reference to "entering into a state of society" turns out, *not* to be a reference, not necessarily anyhow, to men's emerging from a state of nature into society. The document speaks, rather, of entering into *a* state of society, not into *the* state of society, which could just as easily mean moving, as the Virginians were in the act of doing, from an old state of society into a new one. As for the reference to "nature," Locke was in fact a Johnnie-come-very-lately in the history of Western man's speculation about law that is *natural* to man, about man's duties and rights under natural law: Western man, that is, had long been familiar with the idea—it is as old as Augustine—that there are limits to the kind of submission a man can rightly offer up to any earthly government. If we pursue the document a little further, we see that the rights the Virginians proceed to name are old friends of ours, well known and articulated before Locke ever wrote. The rights named by the Virginians under "namely" are precisely "the enjoyment of life, and liberty, with the means of acquiring and possessing property, and pursuing and obtaining happiness and safety," which is recognizably a rewrite of the passage we have already examined briefly in a document that preceded Locke by several decades. Moreover, it is a passage that says nothing that would not have been acceptable to Locke's great teacher Hooker, who certainly was not a Lockean, or to Hooker's great teacher St. Thomas Aquinas. Finally, and a very crucial point, the Virginia Declaration makes a further statement about the "inherent rights" that, for reasons we will readily understand, we hear of far less often in the official literature than the supposedly Lockean statements we have already noticed. The rights, the Declaration begins by saying, are rights that pertain not to all men, not to individuals, but to the "good people of Virginia," and pertain to them precisely as "the basis and foundation of government." But at this point we must again pause, this time to answer a very sensible objection that will have occurred to the reader: What is the difference between rights that pertain to "the people" and rights that pertain to "all men [as individuals]"? This is not only a sensible objection, but it brings us to the very heart of the matter before us.

Let us be very clear about the logic of the objection, which is based to a large extent on the logic of those brought up on the official literature. The people, it says, is made up of *individuals* and *individuals* are what count. To speak the truth of the matter, indeed, there is no such thing as the people, unless you mean by it a collection of individuals. In other words, "the people" is an abstraction, which possesses only a constructive reality; to speak therefore of the "rights of the people," the rights of all men, and the rights of individuals, is simply to say the same thing in three different ways. *How*, then, the objection concludes, can you suggest that there could be a right of the people that is not a right of the individuals who make up the people, and thus of each and every individual?

Now this is compelling logic for persons who have fallen under the spell of Locke, which for most purposes is the same thing as the spell of the official literature—compelling, if for no other reason, because it presupposes or reflects a metaphysics and epistomology of which, you may be sure, we shall not soon hear the last. In light of our purpose, which is an understanding of the American political tradition, we must content ourselves by answering as follows: All that may be right as rain; it may be true that rights inhere only in individuals. But our ancestors, even as late as the Virginia Declaration, did not so understand it. Their logic runs rather as follows: There are indeed rights of individuals (life, liberty, property, happiness, safety) ; those rights ought to be protected, and a good government will, within the limits of the possible, protect them, but that raises the questions: What *is* good government? What is the basis and foundation of such a government? These questions were very much on the minds of the Virginians as we can clearly see by glancing again at the passage in which they

define the very task at hand. Their immediate concern is with
the rights that pertain *to the good people of Virginia*. And we
do not overburden the language of the document by noting
that it so much as tells us that the rights of all individuals will
be safest if *first* the rights of the people are assured, and above
all the right or rights of the people *to govern themselves*, that
is, the very right that we have watched emerging in America
from the Mayflower Compact through the Body of Liberties.
There are, in other words, rights of the people that are *not*
mere shorthand expressions for the rights of individuals; and
we understand more clearly than ever before why we have not
been encountering, in our canvass of the tradition, claims to
rights on the part of individuals that prove to be claims to
rights *against* the legislature. Most important of all, we see,
that the Virginia Declaration, far from being anything particularly novel, falls right within the traditional symbolization
as we have come to know and understand it.

It does, indeed, specify rights that are rights of individuals
(although, curiously, it also tends to avoid the word "rights").
But—and this much we would expect from our previous inqui-
ries—these turn out to be rights "against" the courts of law and
the executive, that is, the so-called "common law rights": The
right of an accused man to know what he is accused of, to be
confronted with his accusers, to call favorable witnesses, to
enjoy speedy trial by an impartial jury, to refuse to testify
against himself. On the negative side, it guarantees against
excessive bail, excessive fines, cruel and unusual punishment,
unreasonable searches and seizures, and standing armies.
Then, finally, on the positive side, a further list of rights: to
trial by jury in civil suits, and—so it appears at first glance—
to freedom of the press (a matter that we will come back to
shortly).

Yet, for all of this, the main business of the Declaration, as
its inherent logic indicates, is the further differentiation of a

symbol we already had in hand before our arrival in Virginia, "better ordering" understood as a matter of self-government by the people. Government, it says, is instituted for the "common benefit, protection, and security, of the people," and for "producing the greatest happiness and safety." This, of course, is our old Mayflower friend, the "general Good," now differentiated into almost the form in which it turns up in the Preamble of the Constitution. All power is vested in, and so derived from, the *people*, so that officials are the people's trustees and responsible to them—as we have seen them to be, by implication, in Massachusetts. This very idea will in due course become a basic, though tacit, principle of the Constitution. When, the document continues, a government "shall be found"—our old Mayflower friend "thought to be" —"inadequate or contrary" to the purposes named, "a majority of the community hath an indubitable, inalienable, and indefeasible right [one of the few cases in which the word "right" is used, but, clearly, a right of the people, now concerned as acting by majority vote, another of our old friends] to reform, alter, or abolish it, in such manner as shall be judged most conducive to the public weal" (which again is one of our old friends "thought to be meet and convenient for the general Good," though now highly differentiated). These provisions of the Virginia Declaration are clearly the core of Article V of our Constitution which gives the majority of the American people the right in question.

No public office, we are told, should be "hereditary"—a new specification, but clearly a differentiation out of the electoral arrangements we encountered a century earlier; and, as we know, all offices in the 1789 Constitution are either elective or appointive. Legislative, executive, and judicial powers, the document continues, should be in separate and distinct hands which, again, is a specification already present, potentially, in the Body of Liberties. Executive and legislative offices should be rotated, vacancies being supplied by "frequent, certain, and regular elections"—again a further differentiation of the Massachusetts differentiation of the Mayflower "better ordering," and one that will turn up in due course in the Philadelphia Constitution. The power of suspending laws, or their execution, shall be exercised only by consent of the representatives of the people, because such power exercised without that consent is injurious to the "rights" of "the people." This is a new specification, but clearly a differentiation out of the Mayflower claim to a capacity, on the part of the signers, to "enact laws, etc." But once again, though a new specification, this too will be incorporated into the Constitution.

What does all this add up to? At least this much: This listing of *rights of the people* that comes to us with the Virginia Declaration shows that the American people have arrived, already, in 1776, at the conception of *democratic government* that is embodied in the greatest of the post-1776 symbols, namely, the Constitution. We at least begin to understand why the Framers of the Constitution opposed the incorporation in it of a bill of rights, and did so on the grounds that it was already a bill of rights. The Constitution incorporated, lock, stock, and barrel, the Declaration's list of "rights of the people," although it omits, as if by conscious intention, the *individual* rights of the Virginia Declaration. As we shall see, the Framers stick to the primary meaning of "rights" in the Virginia Declaration, which has to do with individual rights only at second remove, and even then not as rights "against" the legislature—rights, that is, that the legislature is forbidden to infringe or violate. They stick, and let us emphasize this, to a conception of "rights" that has evolved precisely out of the Mayflower symbols to the extent that they are American symbols, not English symbols. They stick, in short, to a conception of rights that we now see to be the rights of Americans, not Englishmen—unless someone wants to argue that the rights of the Englishmen in 1776 included the right to self-government of the kind that is embodied in the Virginia Declaration. This, we take it, nobody is about to do.

What about freedom of the press which we mentioned in passing? Is it not an individual right and even one that restricts the power of the legislature? If we look only to the text of the Virginia Declaration, we see at once (surprising as it may seem to many) there is no foundation for any such claim. "Freedom of the press," it says, "is one of the great bulwarks of liberty, and can never be restrained but by despotic governments."[4] At most the statement simply affirms a principle or maxim of good government; one that would have to be drastically altered or re-written to confer a legal right to individual citizens. Indeed, if we look a second time at the document, we find that it does not use the word "right" except when it is speaking of a right of the people. What is more, we find that when we come to the matter of "excessive bail," another of the so-called rights, the very same language is used. What the document tells us is that "excessive bail" *ought* not to be required. The same terminology is used with respect to unreasonable searches and seizures (or, as the Declaration puts it, searches and seizures by "general warrant") which, again, *ought* not to be permitted. One might say that the authors of the Declaration seem to be very cautious when they approach the area of what we, today, call individual rights. They only specify the "purest" and most procedural of the common law rights which, in effect, come down to being rights against the courts and administration. For instance, "a man,"

---

[4] Let us note first the "positioning" of this "right." It is to be found in section 12 of the 16 sections which compose the Virginia Bill of Rights. Also, pay close attention to the language of this injunction, if we may call it that. What is more important, we do not find such language, equivocal in nature, used with respect to the injunctions of the first eleven sections of the Virginia Bill of Rights. We will say more about this in Chap. 7 which is on the national Bill of Rights.

that is, each individual, "hath a right" to know what he is accused of, to confront hostile witnesses, to summon friendly witnesses, to be tried speedily by jury, to refuse to testify against himself. But, in this very sentence, covering matters which *we* now regard as personal or individual liberties or rights, the authors of the Declaration do not use the word "right" in the same manner as we do today. What we find in this connection is "no man [can] be deprived of his liberty, except by the *law of the land* or the judgement of his peers"—which, as we should expect from the tradition as we now know it, puts the matter of "liberty" right up to the legislature, and so becomes an affirmation of legislative supremacy. Moreover, to come back to freedom of the press, we know from the first chapter of this book that freedom of the press had, in those days, a meaning that made of it also an affirmation of legislative supremacy: Freedom of the press was freedom to publish within the limits set by the law of seditious libel, which again puts the matter up to the legislature. We are still far from the idea of legally enforceable individual rights that must be respected by the representative assembly. We will have occasion to say more, much more, about legislative supremacy in our chapter on the Bill of Rights.

Two provisions of the Virginia Declaration of Rights warrant our attention in this context. First, the apparent—but as we shall see merely apparent—affirmation of a right of all men, that is, an individual right, to the suffrage. Here, too, we find ourselves in a different world of discourse from that of the individual rights as the official literature usually explains them. If we look hard enough we see that it is not all men who have a right to the suffrage, but merely such men as have given "sufficient evidence of permanent common interest with, and attachment to, the community"—clearly an invitation to the legislature to decide, with an eye to the general good, who may vote and who may not, a power that, under the Constitution,

American legislatures continue to exercise, on condition that they can convince the courts that they are not acting arbitrarily. Perhaps it is not too much to say that the authors of the Virginia Declaration, once they move away from the area of procedural rules in courts of law, assume that an individual has rights only on pain of having performed certain *duties,* certain obligations, which—let us say it again—it is the business of the legislature to define. The Declaration puts us right back with the Connecticut and Massachusetts solution: A man's legal rights are, in general, the rights vouchsafed to him by the representative assembly—which, like the Lord of the Scriptures, giveth and taketh away.

We must, therefore, ask ourselves once again, Are we to understand that the legislature is being invited to do what it pleases, to improvise its own standards, to, in effect, set itself up as God? Here the Virginia Declaration gives us two answers which tell us "No." The legislature is expected— nay, counted upon—to subordinate itself to considerations of humanity, civility, and Christianity. The very words of the document tell us that "no free government, or the blessings of liberty, can be preserved by any people but"—and let us attend carefully to the words employed—"by firm adherence to justice, moderation, temperance, frugality, and virtue, and by frequent recurrence to fundamental principles." This is a reiteration of, at the deepest level of symbolization, the Massachusetts appeal to the political and moral philosophy of the Great Tradition of the West. We see once again our old friend, the symbol of a virtuous people. Clearly the legislature is *not* to set itself up as God. Precisely the function of the Declaration, at its most solemn moment, is to establish the standards which tell us (*a*) the representative assembly is supreme—a proposition which we might expect from our tradition—in the sense that no other *political* authority can challenge or gainsay it; but (*b*) its supremacy, its right or power, is simultaneous with its obligation to subordinate itself to standards *not* of its own making—standards embodying, in Voegelin's phrase, the truth of the soul and of society as that truth has been made known to us by the great philosophers from whom, at this juncture, the Virginia Declaration draws its vocabulary.

Second, we confront another example of what Voegelin means by differentiation of symbols in the course of experience. We notice that something has happened between Massachusetts and Virginia to the symbol of "Christianity," whose continuity through the pre-1789 documents we have noted. "Government" is not mentioned in the paragraph that the Declaration devotes to this topic. More: The paragraph devoted to Christianity stands in juxtaposition with—indeed, follows hard upon—a paragraph in which the authors had every opportunity to mention Christianity in connection with government and, so it seems at least, deliberately passed up the opportunity. One might say that the Virginia Declaration drives a *wedge* between philosophy, which is the symbol to which it appeals when it speaks of justice, moderation, etc., and religion; and, with recognizably symbolic intent, drains the latter, religion, off for separate treatment. We should attend carefully to the language used, at least in order to decide whether we are to mark this as a new turn of the road in our tradition.

The authors of the Declaration do not, we perceive at once, understand or interpret themselves as less Christian, less committed to the truth of the soul and of society as that truth comes to us through Revelation, than, say, the signers of the Mayflower Compact. The Christian religion, they affirm, is the duty which "we," that is, all men, all individuals, owe "to our Creator." "We"—that is, all men, all individuals—have a "mutual duty," they affirm further, "to practice Christian forbearance, love, and charity, towards each other." This we recognize at once as a statement on the level of private, not public ethics, if for no other reason than the matter of governmental or public ethics was amply dealt with in the preceding paragraph. What is affirmed, one might say, is the duty of all Virginians to obey the Ten Commandments plus, over and above the Ten, the Eleventh Commandment, the commandment to love one another. But there is no suggestion that, as in Massachusetts, it is the business of government to enforce the mutual duty in question, or even—to recur to the Mayflower Compact—to glorify God and advance the faith. In other words, the confusion that we noticed back in Massachusetts has been dispelled, and we are on the threshold of the idea, which in due course will become explicit in *The Federalist*, of a Christian *society* with a secular, that is precisely *not* religious, form of government.

The wedge we have been talking about turns out to be a wedge not so much between philosophy and religion (though to some degree it is that) , but a wedge between the sphere of government and the sphere of society. The Christian religion is to govern the relations between Virginians out in society, but is, *as* religion, given no special status in the area of law and coercion. Indeed, the Declaration goes on to say, as on that showing we should expect it to, that the duty we owe to our Creator, and the manner of discharging it, "can be directed only by reason and conviction, *not by force or violence*" [5]— that is, as we understand it, not by government. In the sphere of government, in short, religion is to be given the status it enjoys in the Constitution, which is to say *no* status at all. And it does not seem that we go too far when we say, doubling back to our question as to where the American tradition *begins*: The Mayflower symbols, in this area at least, have arrived— even before the Declaration of Independence—at their definitive American differentiation, and done so in the course of an evolution that we can study only on *this* side of the Atlantic.

[5] Emphasis added.

But having said this, let us repeat that the authors of the Virginia Declaration did *not* understand themselves as less Christian than the authors of the Body of Liberties. It is *not* that the authors of the Virginia Declaration, seemingly taking issue with the authors of the Body of Liberties, understand the commonwealth to be other than a Christian commonwealth. But they do understand a Christian commonwealth to be a different sort of thing from what it was in Massachusetts; in the very act of symbolically disestablishing the Christian religion, by separating it from American government, they establish it as the religion, the public truth, of American society, a status which (we believe) it continues to enjoy. We must not, then, suppose ourselves to be entering the intellecutal and spiritual world of some of our Supreme Court justices, the more so as we find the Declaration going on to say: "All men are equally entitled to the free exercise of religion, according to the dictates of conscience." Only by wrenching these words out of context could we get out of them a "right" claimed by atheists and agnostics—a "right," that is, to the free exercise of irreligion. The very words we have quoted above follow the declaration that religion is a duty that every man owes to his Creator and, to boot, they are preceded by the word "therefore." The "right" to free exercise of religion emerges, in short, as a correlative of the duty to worship God. In the context of the Virginia Declaration, it can have no other meaning. Nor do we think—and this will seem heretical to some—that the framers of our First Amendment entertained a different view.

CHAPTER V

The Declaration
of Independence:
A Derailment?

We now take up the most difficult and undoubtedly the most controversial of our tasks: the symbolism and so the meaning of the Declaration of Independence in the context of the American tradition.[1] Before we discuss its place in the tradition, a few preliminary comments are in order. One obvious matter—so obvious, in fact, it hardly seems to merit our attention or emphasis—is that the Declaration of Independence should be read for what it purports to be. We begin at this point because the official literature tends to overlook the obvious: The document's primary purpose is to announce publicly the severing of those "bands" that had, until July 4, 1776, tied us morally and legally to Great Britain. *That* is the purpose of the document and *that*, we submit, should be foremost in the minds of those who read and interpret it.

The Declaration begins with these words: "*The unanimous Declaration of the thirteen united States of America.*" The words are in themselves important because we see at once that, contrary to what we may have been taught in our institutions of higher learning, there is no pretense as of this moment that we are, legally speaking or otherwise, one people or nation. Why, indeed, would this phraseology be used if the participants felt the colonies should be regarded as one? The thirteen

---

[1] We use as our test the Declaration as reproduced in Poore, I, 1–6.

states are "united" for the purpose of declaring their independence, and so far as we can see no other purpose is even so
much as mentioned in the remainder of the document. The
word "unanimous" in this connection is also revealing. It clearly suggests that the Declaration could have been something
other than unanimous; but, beyond any question, the document takes on added force simply because of this unanimity.

Immediately following this very brief opening statement,
we find the following, which more clearly tells us what the
"unanimous Declaration" is about. The well-known words
(though hardly as well known as those of the paragraph immediately following) are these: "When in the Course of
human events, it becomes necessary for one people to dissolve
the political bands which have connected them with another,
and to assume among the Powers of the earth, the separate and
equal station to which the Laws of Nature and of Nature's God
entitle them, a decent respect to the opinions of mankind requires that they should declare the causes which impel them
to the separation." This passage taken in isolation could be
interpreted to mean that we already regard ourselves as one
people or nation; or, short of this, by this Declaration we are
announcing to the world our "oneness." But this phraseology,
let us remember, is to be read in light of the preceding sentence which clearly permits the form of expression used without any ambiguity. If there be any doubts on this point, the
last paragraph ought to dispel them. We will quote it and then
point out what we think to be two of its more significant
points.

We, therefore, the Representatives of the united States of America, in General Congress, Assembled, appealing to the Supreme
Judge of the world for the rectitude of our intentions, do, in the
Name, and by the Authority of the good People of these Colonies,
solemnly publish and declare, That these United Colonies are, and
of Right ought to be Free and Independent States; that they are

Absolved from all Allegiance to the British Crown, and that all political connection between them and the State of Great Britain, is and ought to be totally dissolved; and that as *Free and Independent States*, they have full Power to levy War, conclude Peace, contract Alliances, establish Commerce, and *to do all other Acts and Things which independent States may of right do.* And for the support of this Declaration, with a firm reliance on the Protection of the Divine Providence, we mutually pledge to each other our Lives, our Fortunes and our sacred Honor.[2]

First: We cannot help but note the invocation of the supreme symbols of our tradition. The signers appeal to the "Supreme Judge . . . for the rectitude of" their "intentions" and make it quite clear that they do so "in the Name, and by the Authority of the good People of these Colonies." Such language, though a bit different, is not foreign to our ears. The paragraph also contains other phrases that would place it very much in the mainstream of the tradition: The signers "solemnly publish and declare" their independence; they do place a "firm reliance on the Protection of Divine Providence" for the justness of their case and their course of action; and above all, they realize the very seriousness of their undertaking for they pledge their "Lives," "Fortunes," and—what may be most important—their "sacred Honor."

Second: We see from the text that we are not a united people. The text speaks of "Free and Independent States" and so far as we can tell they are endowed with all those powers we normally attribute to sovereign states. Still, apart from the fact that the states or colonies are united in their Declaration of Independence from Britain, there is another sense in which they can be said to be united, for such a Declaration would only be possible if there were an existing forum for the formulation and issuance of the Declaration, as indeed there was. This fact itself indicates that the colonists were of

2 Emphasis added.

kindred hearts (or, at least, thought themselves to be) on some issues and problems confronting them. But beyond this, and far more important in terms of our subsequent history, lurks another matter still very latent but potentially highly explosive: When, on what issues, and in what sense are we to consider ourselves as independent states in the sense that the Declaration declares? To be sure, we can only partially perceive this problem on the basis of the text itself, but we know enough to see that it will subsequently become an issue of major proportions. Let us leave aside this point, for we will return to it in the next chapter.

Other major segments of the Declaration fit very well into the tradition as we have described it to this point in history.

(a) We find that most of the document is devoted to an enumeration of a bill of particulars directed (and this is not an uninteresting point) against the king of Great Britian.[3] These particulars, or the reasons for separation, constitute the long middle section of the document (often overlooked, particularly by those who like to dwell ad nauseam on the second paragraph), stretching from the third paragraph to the third from the last paragraph. And what do we glean from this bill of particulars? For starters, the document tells us so much: "The history of the present King of Great Britain is a history of repeated injuries and usurpations, all having in direct object the establishment of an absolute Tyranny over these States." The words "tyrant" and "tyranny" are frequently used to describe the action of the king, and the language of the third paragraph from the end is somewhat remarkable, in light of relativist claims that tyranny is, after all, a subjective

---

3 We suspect, Carl Becker (another of the official "custodians") notwithstanding, that the colonists had a pretty healthy respect for legislatures and processes of representation embodied therein. Therefore, they were reluctant to single out Parliament for blame. Only in the second to the last paragraph does Parliament come under attack. And, then, compared with the treatment accorded the king, it is very mild.

condition. We quote: "A Prince, whose character is thus marked by every act which may define a Tyrant, is unfit to be the ruler of a free People." Yes, the language is a bit equivocal only to the extent that they accuse him of *acting* like a tyrant, but there is no getting around the text; they did believe they were in the midst of tyranny, and throughout they make this quite emphatic.

(b) What precisely has the king done that is tyrannical? The Declaration is abundantly clear on this point, and we can only presume that further specifications could be provided if called for. Upon examination a number of them are precisely what we would expect on the basis of our previous analysis of the tradition. At least eleven involve violations (seven of which are the first mentioned) of our supreme symbol as a people: namely, *self-government* through *deliberative* processes. For example: "He has refused his Assent to Laws, the most wholesome and necessary for the public good." Or, "He has dissolved Representative Houses repeatedly, for opposing with manly firmness his invasions of the rights of the people." Or again, "He has refused to pass other Laws for the accommodation of large districts of people, unless those people would relinquish the right of Representation in the Legislature, a right inestimable to them and formidable to tyrants only." Particulars of this nature abound; but what is most significant is that we find that repeated and continued violation of our basic commitment as a people comes to be a matter of being tyrannical which, at the very least, gives us some appreciation of the depth of our traditional commitment.

Still another category of grievances has to do with certain transgressions involving some of our basic symbolizations that over time, as we have shown, were well along in the process of differentiation—at least to a point where violations of their strictures could be easily identified. Here we speak of separation of powers, at least as it was understood by the colonists.

"He has obstructed the Administration of justice, by refusing his Assent to Laws for establishing Judiciary Powers." And what would seem to be worse, given our subsequent differentiation of this symbol at the national level, "He has made judges dependent on his Will alone, for the tenure of their offices, and the amount and payment of their salaries." In a somewhat related vein—and this issue is still very much with us even today—"He has affected to render the Military independent of and superior to the Civil Power." Again we could go on. We note here only that we find nothing that does not square with that tradition of the colonists as we have presented it. Quite the contrary: We should expect them to speak in this very fashion and to cite examples of the nature and kind they do.

A third category of particulars involves our most fundamental commitment of all: The king has acted in a totally barbarous manner, but, what is worse, he has committed acts that outrage the sensibilities and morals of a virtuous people. To wit: "He has plundered our seas, ravaged our Coasts, burnt our towns, and destroyed the lives of our people." And the following passage, as hard as it is to believe, is even stronger: "He is at this time transporting large armies of foreign mercenaries to compleat the works of death, desolation and tyranny, already begun with circumstances of Cruelty and perfidy scarcely paralleled in the most barbarous ages, and totally unworthy of the Head of a civilized nation." Scarcely any language could be stronger, and we have every reason to believe that such a forceful statement, employing the terms it does, without any qualification, equivocation, or modification, could not possibly have been forthcoming unless the signers were deeply imbedded in a tradition.[4] Moreover, the signers speak

4 We believe it was a tradition, moreover, embedded in Western political thinking to the extent that tyranny was a meaningful term. All of this is in sharp contrast to our modern-day positivists and relativists (e.g., Dahl and T. D.

in terms of a "civilized nation" in a manner to suggest that they have a pretty fixed notion—very much again unlike so many contemporary intellectuals—of what does constitute the behavior of a "civilized" state, as well as what constitutes the behavior of a state something less than civilized.

A few more comments about the Declaration and then we will tackle what seems to be the more important problems it presents for the understanding of our American tradition. The Declaration has been characterized by some as a "conservative" document, in large part for reasons we have already specified: It does pay due homage to the opinions of mankind, does indicate that this is a very serious undertaking, does specify the reasons and justifications for the undertaking, and so forth. But, for all of this, it is misleading to characterize the document as conservative. What we have is a document that reaffirms the central truths of our tradition as they were perceived at this point in our history.[5] The second paragraph would seem to make this clear. After setting forth the doctrine that there are "unalienable rights" ("Life, Liberty, and the pursuit of Happiness"), the Declaration continues: "That to secure these rights, Governments are instituted among Men, deriving their just powers from the consent of the governed, That whenever any Form of Government becomes destructive of these ends, it is the Right of the People to alter or to abolish it, and to institute a new Government, laying its foundation on such principles and organizing its powers in such form, as to them shall seem most likely to effect their Safety and Happiness." This passage merits our close attention. In the first place, the signers are speaking about a system which has been *"destructive"* of these ends; that has, and we do not strain the

Weldon), who tell us that tyranny amounts to nothing more than a significant group of the population being highly displeased with the course of events.

[5] See on this point Kendall and Carey, "Towards a Definition of Conservatism," *Journal of Politics* (May, 1964). Off of our analysis we would have to call the drafters reactionary, rather than conservative.

text, not merely shown poor judgment about how to advance these and like ends, but has positively sought to violate them. For this reason, among others, the signers are capable of speaking in the emphatic and unambiguous terms they do in describing the king and the system. More importantly, one of the "Rights of the People" (and note well it is a *right of the people*) which is perhaps paramount in the context of the Declaration is that of altering or abolishing a government which acts so callously or outrageously. And, as the text indicates, an important ingredient of this right is that of instituting a "new Government, laying its foundation on such principles and organizing its powers in such form, *as to them shall seem most likely to effect* their *Safety and Happiness.*" [6] With this expression alone we are reminded of the words of the Mayflower Compact wherein the signers speak of a "better ordering" and a pledge to make "just and equal laws" which shall be "thought" most "meet and convenient" for the "general Good of the community." The signers of the Declaration seem to be merely reaffirming that which is central to our tradition. The promise held out is all that the signers can hold out: They do not claim that any new government which might result from the Declaration *will* provide for the "Safety and Happiness" of the constituents but it will be one that "shall seem" to the people "*most likely* to effect their Safety and Happiness." [7]

But what principles and organization of governmental power are most likely to bring about the desired conditions? Surely, off of what we have said in the previous chapters, we could make some pretty shrewd guesses. However, the Declaration does not deal with this matter nor should we, in light of what we have said, expect it to. Its purpose, we say once again, was

6 Emphasis added. We now find ourselves with this expression in the midst of our basic and traditional symbols as a people.

7 Emphasis added.

"to dissolve the political bands" which heretofore connected the colonists with Great Britain. What is important in this connection is that (a) we can anticipate at some future date the states and even the nation, if and when the people see fit, will engage in some sort of deliberative process to establish that form of government which is conducive to the ends cited;[8] and (b) the Declaration itself gives us no guidance on how or in what ways such governments ought to be built. Put otherwise, in no sense can the Declaration be considered a manual for the construction of new governments, and those who prefer to read it as such had better go back to the text. The only morality of the Declaration on this score is that the people retain the right to institute a new government on such principles and in such a way as to them seems most conducive to the goals of safety and happiness. In this regard, it is only slightly different from the Virginia Bill of Rights which declared: "That government is, or ought to be, instituted for the common benefit, protection and security of the people, nation, or community; . . . and that, when any government shall be found inadequate or contrary to these purposes, a *majority* or the *community* have an *indubitable* right to reform, alter, or abolish, in such a manner as shall be judged most conducive to the public weal." [9]

Clearly, as our comments and analysis indicate, we do not, as so many are wont to do, have to recur to the John Lockes or the *philosophes* of the so-called age of enlightenment to explain the purposes, symbolization, and language of the document. In fact, to do so, we maintain, cannot but help to lead to endless confusion and a basic misunderstanding of the basic symbols of the American political tradition. To illustrate our

---

[8] This is precisely what our Constitution was intended and designed to do. Much of the discussion which immediately follows is based on Willmoore Kendall's "Equality: Commitment or Ideal?" *Phalanx* (Fall, 1967) .

[9] Emphasis added.

point, let us consider the first part of the second paragraph—
that part of the document best known to both school boys and
the custodians of our lore—which reads: "We hold these truths
to be self-evident, that all men are created equal, that they are
endowed by their Creator with certain inalienable Rights."
It is precisely here that we find the source of the major controversy surrounding the Declaration and its meaning in our
tradition. More specifically, it is the "all men are created
equal" clause that has over the years been interpreted in such
a way as to cause a derailment in our tradition.[10]

To show this we need only jump ahead four score and seven
years from the signing of the Declaration to Lincoln's famed
Gettysburg address.[11] Its opening words are: "Four score and
seven years ago, our fathers brought forth on this continent, a
new nation, conceived in Liberty, and dedicated to the proposition that all men are created equal." All the words here are
key words, and we can deduce from them at least four fundamental propositions: first, that the United States, as a nation
was born in 1776; second, the United States was conceived in
liberty; third, the United States in the very act of being born
dedicated itself to the overriding proposition that "all men
are created equal," which we may also take to be our basic
commitment as a people; and fourth, our basic commitment
has not been modified or repudiated in the eighty-seven years
between the time of the Declaration and the Gettysburg address.

In this and the next chapter, we will take up these proposi-

10 The derailment has been caused by intellectuals and men in public life
who have seen in this phrase a "mandate" for action which involves, *inter alia*,
a restructuring of American society so as to produce a condition of equality.
This belief in a mandate is so dominant in our intellectual and political circles
that we could not possibly cite all those who have at one time or another publicly professed it. We can say that, in one fashion or another, every major presi-
dential candidate in recent times has subscribed to it.

11 We have taken our text from Richard N. Current (ed), *The Political
Thought of Abraham Lincoln* (Indianapolis: Bobbs-Merrill, 1967), 284–85.

tions, though not in the order we have presented them. However, a few words seem appropriate concerning what we can term the theoretical presumptions which clearly seem to underlie this and other parts of Lincoln's address. He speaks not merely of a commitment but also of a commitment that is *binding*, a commitment that *ought* to be honored and fulfilled. Beyond this, the commitment is binding on the nation or, we might say, all of the people. Shortly we will endeavor to set forth the logic or the reasoning behind any such contentions. For our present purpose it is sufficient to note that he *does* speak in these terms. We have good reason to believe that Lincoln probably would not quibble with the proposition that nations do have commitments in the form of basic symbols that do spell out the over-riding purposes and obligations of a nation. For our part, we find nothing to fault in any such presumption—our point throughout has been that a people comes to understand itself through an understanding of its supreme symbols and basic commitments. Lacking an understanding and perception of its commitments, a people are rudderless, so much so that when faced with crises which demand resolution, they speak with so many tongues that any answer to the pressing question, "What shall we do?", is virtually impossible to come by. And, in turn, to answer this question means, perforce, that they must answer the prior questions, "Who and what are we as people?". Surely, all of this must have troubled Lincoln and does help account for the language and approach he does use. We repeat: Lincoln's language off of the opening paragraph certainly seems to suggest that he entertained such a view and we have no quarrel with him on this matter.

Still another presumption is this: Our commitment as a people to an overriding purpose of supreme symbol (for this is what it comes down to in Lincoln's address) is a hereditary one that presumably we, as a people or nation, could repudiate. However, until such time—through, we must assume, the very same processes by which we made our original commitment—we are bound to act in fulfillment of the commitment made by our forefathers. Now any such presumption involves us with a problem well known to students of political theory. We may appropriately call it the problem of political obligation which arises as a very special problem for political philosophers whose theories are based on the doctrine of consent. The matter can be stated in the following terms: Suppose that one generation establishes a political society or, more importantly, enunciates the supreme symbols for a political society (the two, as we know, can go hand in hand). Let us further assume that there is genuine consensus in this undertaking. What happens then, when and if at some later date, some of the participants come forth and say: "We want out of our commitment. We now find that living up to our commitment is proving more costly than we imagined."? Or, and this may well be the case: "You (that is, the society) have interpreted the commitments in such a way that you are now asking me to acquiesce in policies that, in my judgment, contravene the principles upon which we did agree." A consent theorist such as Rousseau, for example, would respond in roughly the following fashion: "But you promised—in the very act of giving your consent you promised—and we now call upon you to keep your promise, that is, not begrudge the sacrifice that our kind of society, with this form of government and this purpose or set of purposes, now demands of you." Such reasoning seems to bind individuals and, simultaneously, places all the blame for punishment on the shoulder of those who fail to live up to the commitments as defined by society.

The situation is, understandably, more complicated as a people moves through history. What do we answer those (e.g., the great-great-grand-children of those who presumably did set forth our basic commitments) who argue: "This commitment or those commitments are not of my doing. I am not responsible for having made them. How can anyone say that I am obligated? Am I to be governed by the Dead Hand of the Past?" Answers to this are provided by the consent theorists and implicitly by those who drafted the Philadelphia Constitution. They run as follows: "You have indeed consented by remaining within our recognized territorial limits, by affording yourself the protection of our government, by exercising those privileges and rights which our system legally confers upon you and the very benefits you derive from the compliance of others in the exercise of these rights. To be sure, you have only tacitly agreed to these commitments but, nonetheless, this amounts to your consent, tacit though it be." The obvious rejoinders to this line of argument are usually something as follows: "The tacit consent to which you refer is certainly not a matter of deliberate choice. Your contention, off at the end, is based upon my mere physical presence in the United States and there was no effective choice but to obey." To this we can respond, consistent with the consent theory: "But you *do* have a choice. You can leave the territorial limits of the country (as, indeed, some have done) and find a more congenial society whose basic commitments are either more to your liking or less offensive to you. Nor will it do you much good to say that you can't find a more congenial society: that is, one whose values correspond with yours. All this would show is that our society is better than others and that our system is, if nothing else, better than any other—a fact which should be proof enough that we are not as unreasonable as you contend." But more can and should be said on this point in the context of the American tradition. In our tradition we can, at least, say: "You have still another alternative far less bleak than that we have presented. One of our basic commitments is spelled out in Article V of the Constitution which specifies the means by which you can change our basic commitment. What you have to do in order to bring the world around to your image is simply amend the Constitution through procedures and processes that are not any more stringent than those by which the Constitution was itself adopted in the first place. And, if you are able to overturn our basic constitutional commitments through these prescribed processes, the new commitments must be honored. Those who disagree with the changes must face the very arguments we have set forth for honoring our present commitments."

We are in a position now to return to Lincoln's speech and to certain of the basic *propositions* contained in the first paragraph of the Gettysburg Address. Lincoln's propositions, we submit, are compelling not because they stand on their merits (something we can and will show) but rather because of the presumptions that underlie them and even allow him to speak in such terms. The presumptions *are* very much a part of our tradition. Because they are, we should not allow him—not at least without some probing inquiry—to "steal" the game, that is, to accept his interpretation of the Declaration, its place in our history, and its meaning as "true," "correct," and "binding." Put otherwise, Lincoln's words are revered because they seem to stand as a succinct and, in their own way, eloquent statement of the American tradition. They take on their essential meaning largely because they are couched in a language that only makes sense to those reared and nurtured in a tradition accustomed to tacitly accepting those premises which undergird it. In the vernacular, "He talks like one of us." For this reason, we suspect, American scholarship has overlooked what we must label the Lincolnian heresies.

(a) In Lincoln's view the Declaration enjoys what we can best term a *constitutional status*. He so much as informs us that the "new nation" of the United States of America was established with the signing of the Declaration and that it is to this document we must look if we are to understand our origins and thus the meaning of our political experience as a people, organized for action in history and capable of defining its appointed role in history. Lincoln does not say, nor could he, that the Declaration tells everything that we would want to know about our tradition and commitments as a people. Nevertheless, it is to this document that he refers for the identification of our supreme commitment. And the very notion that we are honor-bound to preserve and advance that commitment surely means that the document does enjoy *constitutional status*—for this, above all else, is precisely the *raison d'etre* for documents of this nature.

Yet the facts in more ways than one do not bear out Lincoln's view of the Declaration. The "four score and seven years" of Lincoln's speech does put us back to the Declaration. But why should we take Lincoln's word about our beginning? He might more appropriately have said "three score and fourteen years ago" which would have put us back to 1789, a point in our history that has a far stronger claim to marking the beginnings of our nation. Conceivably, he could have selected any number of dates prior to the Declaration—he might, for example, have selected the year of the Mayflower Compact; though to do so would certainly have blunted the point he seemed intent upon making. For whatever reason, Lincoln is guilty of committing a very serious error, for he fixes our beginning as a people, any way you look at it, either at a point after our beginning or before it. In other words, a claim could be made that the adoption of our Constitution essentially marks our beginning, for at this juncture we did through deliberative processes—far more deliberative, candid, and sober than those surrounding the adoption of the Declaration—set forth our supreme symbols. What is more, the fifty-five at Philadelphia knew precisely what their task or mission was, namely, that of fashioning a new government for the separate thirteen colonies on such foundations and with such processes that would allow for union. Put still otherwise, to speak as Lincoln does about binding commitments off of the Declaration, on the face of it, is not at all convincing for one who wants to argue, as we presume Lincoln would, about obligation in the same sense as the consent theorists. Those who would want to renege on the alleged promises would have more than one reason to say: "We know nothing about the binding commitment you suggest. The document in which you presumably find that commitment does not bind us. It is merely a declaration which states our reasons for separation from Great Britain. It was not intended to be, nor is it, a document which binds us to commitments as a nation and people."

(b) The Declaration of Independence did not, as Lincoln proclaims, establish our independence *as a nation*. Rather, what it did was to establish a baker's dozen of new sovereignties. The record indicates that the states or colonies (whatever one prefers to call them) understood this. Those who think otherwise had best go back to the records. On May 15, 1776, the Continental Congress so much as warns the colonies to prepare for the worst. As the Georgia Assembly put it: "It has been recommended by the said Congress, on the fifteenth of May last, to the respective assemblies and conventions. of the United States, where no government, sufficient to the exigencies of their affairs, hath been hitherto established, to adopt such government as may, in the opinion of the representatives of the people, best conduce to the happiness and safety of their constituents in particular and American in general."[12] The Congress of New Hampshire, responding to the very first recommendation of the Continental Congress, took it upon itself to "use such means and pursue such measures as we should judge best for the public good," [13] and proposed a new constitution which was adopted on January 5, 1776. In

---

12 Poore, I, 378.
13 *Ibid.*, II, 1279.

sum, eleven of the thirteen colonies either at the urgings of the Continental Congress or shortly after the Declaration did establish independent governments (that is, independent of Great Britain). The Constitution of the State of New York, adopted in 1777, even quotes the entire Declaration of Independence as justification for the establishment of its new government.

(c) Let us assume for the moment that the Declaration, as Lincoln would seem to have it, does enjoy a constitutional status so that we can draw from it binding commitments—at least in the sense that we have talked about binding commitments above. Even if this were so, he is still not entitled off of the text of the document to wrench from it a single proposition and make that our supreme commitment. We have only to look at the actual words of the Declaration to see that the only way you can read any such commitment out of it is by first reading it into it. "We," the document reads, "hold these truths to be self-evident, that all men are created equal, that they are endowed by their Creator with certain unalienable Rights, that among these are Life, Liberty, and the pursuit of Happiness." The proposition "that all men are created equal" is but one of at least four propositions. Moreover, the propositions are distinct and in part contradictory; they do not keep house with each other very well. Think only of the endless controversies about how to reconcile the values of liberty and equality.

Nor can we read these propositions either singly or wholly as a statement of goals, purposes, or commitments. When we read the entire text of the Declaration and recall its stated purpose, the best we can say is that governments ought to— and hopefully, all future governments of our making will—

(1) honor and secure the inalienable rights of man; and hence
(2) derive their powers from the consent of the governed.

(d) We can go one step further. Let us grant once again that the Declaration does enjoy constitutional status. Let us also grant that, when all is said and done, the "all men are created equal" clause does represent our most basic commitment as a people. We must then pause to ask, "What does this commitment entail? What does it demand of us?" We could, beyond any doubt, look and ponder over the words at considerable length. Do the drafters really mean "all men"? That is, do they mean it literally in the sense of "every man"? We might say so given the fact that women were seemingly excluded from the most reasonable injunction of any such terminology. However, the assembly that approved the Declaration would not subscribe to the denunciation of slavery that Jefferson sought to include, so that we might be led to believe that the signers were talking of equality of men in a sense far short of that which modern egalitarians hold. Perhaps we can suggest equality before the law. Or could it mean "all men" or even "all men who count" are equal in the eyes of God? Perhaps, even, the value to which we are presumably "dedicated" is meaningless. [See appendix for further discussion of this point.]

We can say this much off the record: The phrase certainly was interpreted in a fashion quite different than our contemporaries interpret it. The Constitution of the State of South Carolina of 1778, in which due acknowledgement of the Declaration is made, declares:

The qualification of electors shall be that every free white man, and no other person, who acknowledges the being of a God, and believes in a future state of rewards and punishments, and who has attained to the age of one and twenty years, and hath been a resident and inhabitant in this State for the space of one whole year before the day appointed for the election he offers to give his vote at, and hath a freehold at least of fifty acres of land, or a town lot, and hath been legally seized and possessed of the same at least six months previous to such election, or hath paid a tax the preceding year, or was taxable the present year, at least six months previous to the said election, in a sum equal to the tax of fifty acres of land, to the support of this government, shall be deemed a person qualified to vote.[14]

The restrictions in many other states were not as severe, but most of them did impose some sort of "property test" which, we may take it, was designed to insure that the electorate did have a "permanent attachment" to the community. And the exclusion of women and slaves in state constitutions written at the time of the Declaration should serve to raise some questions about what the signers of the Declaration did mean by the phrase "all men are created equal." [15] While it is anybody's guess what the signers did mean, we have every reason to believe they certainly did not view it as a new overriding commitment.

And (e) these state constitutions written shortly before and after the Declaration can only be read in the light of our tradition and the commitments we have already noted. Most states, in one fashion or another, subscribe to the New Hampshire dictum, namely, to "use such means and pursue such measures" as to be deemed "best for the public good." [16] The representatives of the state of New York use similar language in their constitution. They feel themselves empowered "to institute and establish such a government as they shall deem best calculated to secure the rights and liberties of the good people of this State." [17] Significantly, Connecticut makes very few changes at all. Its constitution, very short, begins with these words: "The People of this State, being by the Providence of God, free and independent, have the sole and exclu-

14 We here speak of the 1778 Constitution. *Ibid.*, II, 1623.
15 These are questions which we have conspicuously ignored, given our current intellectual and political climate which all but forbids raising them.
16 On this point, one need only read Poore.
17 *Ibid.*, II, 1332.

sive Right of governing themselves as a free, sovereign, and
independent State; and having from their Ancestors derived a
free and excellent Constitution of Government whereby the
Legislature depends on the free and annual Election of the
People, they have the best Security for the Preservation of
their civil and religious Rights and Liberties." [18] In sum,
with only the addition of a few common-law rights, the citizens of Connecticut are content to stick with the Fundamental
Orders. Surely, if any revolution in the American tradition
had occurred—revolution in the sense of new commitments
and symbols—the people of Connecticut were apparently unaware of it.

To fix upon the Declaration and to extract from it our basic
commitment in the manner that Lincoln has done cannot help
but create a distorted picture of our tradition. This alone is a
very serious matter. But what is more, we are now in the process of seeing how it is that a tradition is derailed. Those who
seize upon and stress the "all men are created equal" clause,
quite in keeping with the Lincolnian view of the tradition,
have slowly, and understandably enough, fixed upon the symbol of "equality" as supreme. To be sure, the notions about
what equality means do vary in scope. For some, it is nothing
more than "equality of opportunity." To others, it comes
down to political equality in the sense of one man, one vote.
For still others, however (and this includes many of our contemporary intellectuals and political leaders), the commitment to equality means that government should assume the
role of advancing equality by pursuing policies designed to
make "all men equal" socially, economically, and politically.
As we shall see in due course, we have come to have two traditions: one which holds to a rather extreme view of equality;
the other, an older one, which holds that our supreme symbol is to rule the deliberate sense of the community. This

[18] *Ibid.,* I, 257.

accounts for the fact that we are somewhat schizophrenic today about our tradition. Beyond this is a graver matter; the two traditions are not compatible with one another, and the manifestations of this are quite apparent in our contemporary world.

CHAPTER **VI**

Constitutional Morality
and *The Federalist*

To treat the Constitution and *The Federalist*[1] separately is difficult. The two documents are closely associated in most people's minds, as well they should be, because they come before us in history one upon the other within a very short period of time. Also, as we know very well, *The Federalist* represents an attempt to justify the Constitution in the strongest possible terms in order to meet the objections of its critics and obtain the support necessary for ratification in New York State. For these reasons, treating the two documents together seems reasonable enough. But our reason for lumping them together is of a different order: The Constitution, while specifying the machinery and procedures of our government, gives us few clues as to how, in what manner, and according to what principles we should interpret it or operate under its forms.[2] We know also that the Constitution is susceptible of alternative "readings," and so did the drafters, as we can easily discern from even a cursory reading of what are now fashionably termed the "Antifederalist" writings. The Antifederalists, not without justification, tended—most of them, at any rate—to

---

1 All Federalist quotations are from Jacob E. Cooke (ed.) *The Federalist*, (Cleveland and New York: Meridian Books, 1961).

2 Kendall and Carey, Intro., *The Federalist* (New Rochelle: Arlington House, 1965). In this introduction we set forth at some length the reasons for this contention. Also we explain why *The Federalist* is best read as being the product of a single individual, named "Publius."

draw a pretty extreme picture of what *could* happen under the proposed system: The senators, because of their mode of election and length of office, could well become the "noblemen" of our society and could intrigue among themselves to capture control of the system; the President might well use his control over our armed forces to intimidate both the people and the other branches of government into compliance with his will; and, among other things, the Supreme Court could become an oligarchy.

The Antifederalist writings are in one sense understandable. Imagine this: If we were to present a ball and a bat to a teenager of the 1820's, he might be just a little more than perplexed about what to do with them, the more so as he sought to play any sort of game with the kids next door. However, armed with an instruction booklet on the rules of the game we now call baseball, some of the uncertainties would vanish, particularly with respect to (*a*) what the ball and bat are for and (*b*) what kind of interesting game could be played with them. With the adoption of the Constitution, the situation was somewhat analogous—only somewhat, because, as the fact that the Constitution was adopted so quickly and overwhelmingly attests, the people must have had a pretty fair notion about what the rules of the game were under the proposed Constitution. And this is not surprising because, as we have endeavored to show, the very tradition before us to the time of the Constitution served to make our constitutional structure meaningful. Indeed, most of the Antifederalist writings, though understandable, *are* absurd (to those, at least, who have taken the time to read them) simply because they are "brittle" and tend to interpret our constitutional system in a manner foreign to the context of the tradition. Yet, for all of this, there are questions (surprisingly few of the Antidederalists fixed upon them) that are not answered by the Constitution or the tradition of which it is but a part. *The Federalist,* and this fact is often overlooked in the official literature, provides us with answers to some of our more perplexing questions. In so doing, it urges upon us what can best be termed a "constitutional morality" or, that is, a way of looking at and interpreting the provisions of the Constitution so as to render it a viable instrument capable of fulfilling the purposes stated in the Preamble. Once accepted, such a morality assumes over time something of a binding character; we tend to look upon it as a part of the very Constitution itself which is binding both upon citizens and those who hold positions of authority within our government. And while there are many ways of looking at the Constitution, each with an accompanying morality, Publius' "reading" of the Constitution has gained such wide acceptance over the years that most individuals find it difficult to read the Constitution with an "innocent eye." For instance, the Constitution does not provide for what we call today "judicial review." Nor, on the other hand, does it say that the Supreme Court should not have such powers. The Constitution establishes three branches of government, but it does not say that these branches are "equal and coordinate." Conversely, it does not prohibit the development of our institutions so as to render them "equal and coordinate." For another, Congress, off of the Constitution, seems to be as powerful as any other legislative assembly in the world including the British Parliament. It could, with sufficient majorities in both houses, impeach the President, justices of the courts, and use its power over the purse with an eye to subordinating the courts and the President to its will. But, again, nothing in the Constitution tells Congress to restrain itself, to use the powers at its disposal only in the most critical situations. Or, for still another example, there is nothing that prevents the development of a *plebiscitary* system under the forms of the Constitution—a system in which the people choose between alternative programs, thereby giving to the President and Congress a man-

date which they can ignore only at their peril. Now, to understand the Constitution with respect to these and like matters,
as well as much of our subsequent development as a nation,
one must look to *The Federalist.*

Despite what we have said to this point, certain parts of the
Constitution can be studied separately from *The Federalist.*
The Preamble is, for instance, best read in conjunction with
the Declaration if we are to understand the subsequent derailment of our tradition. The Preamble reads: "We the People
of the United States, in Order to form a more perfect Union,
establish justice, insure domestic Tranquility, provide for the
common defence, promote the general Welfare, and secure
the Blessings of Liberty to ourselves and our Posterity, do ordain and establish this Constitution for the United States of
America." [3] There are a number of things to be said about
this passage:

(*a*) When talking about our commitments as a people, the
words of the Preamble do not seem to flow as readily from the
lips of the custodians of the official literature as those of
the second paragraph of the Declaration. This is somewhat remarkable for the simple reason that if we are to look for any
single statement of our purposes as a nation or people, constituted and organized for action upon the stage of history, it
surely must be in the Preamble. Though we have many times
amended our Constitution, we have not as yet amended the
Preamble which still serves as our finest statement of purpose,
and we should expect, for this reason, that those who would
seek to remind us of our commitments and obligations, or to
enforce these commitments upon wayward segments of the
community, would of necessity have to recur to it.

(*b*) There can be no question either that the Founding
Fathers are establishing a new political order. They "ordain

---

3 With only the slightest of modifications we have used Poore's text.

and establish this Constitution" (and here we vary the order, but without infidelity to the text), "in Order to form a more perfect Union," which means clearly that at this point in time, we did have a union, one as we know, formed by the Articles of Confederation. And the promise held out in the Preamble is *not* a "perfect union" but a "more perfect union." What is clear, however, is that the shortcomings of the Articles are so great and severe that the Articles cannot be merely "overhauled" or amended to secure a "more perfect union." Rather the Articles have to be junked, new purposes and machinery of decision-making established to attain a "more perfect union." And, as we well know, the actions on the part of the Philadelphia founders toward their instructions regarding the Articles of Confederation betrayed an obviously strong belief that "all the king's horses and all the king's men" couldn't render the Articles a viable governing instrument.

(c) The Preamble helps us understand in what ways our "union" is to be "more perfect." The new Constitution will "establish Justice, insure domestic Tranquility," etc. We may fairly assume that the Framers are, in citing those ends and purposes, also emphasizing the weaknesses of government under the Articles, or, to put the matter somewhat differently, are emphasizing those acknowledged purposes of government that have not been fulfilled under the Articles. Now we cannot help but observe that the Preamble's purposes will not keep house with each other any more than those we find in the Declaration. We know—or could readily imagine without the benefit of any experience at all—providing for the "common defence" can well involve sacrifices in terms of our "domestic Tranquility." Countless other conflicts between these stated purposes, which we need not dwell on here, have arisen in the course of our history. But, very much unlike the Declaration, this is not a fatal objection to the Constitution, for in the remainder of the document we find detailed specification of the procedures for the resolution of those conflicts that might arise. And this, of course, is far more than we can say about the Declaration.

Now, for sure, when the Framers speak in the Preamble of "Justice," "domestic Tranquility," "the common defense," and "the Blessings of Liberty," they are promising us a good deal more than when they speak of "a more perfect Union." Justice, for example, seems to be just plain justice, without any qualifications; and they speak about the blessings of liberty *as if* these blessings were known well enough that they could be *secured*. The shift of language can certainly be regarded as something of a foreboding. It would seem that justice, domestic tranquility, etc., are symbols whose content and meanings are well enough known so that the need for elaboration and qualification does not seem at all imperative.

Not so when they speak about "Union." They promise only that—we take it through processes established by the Constitution and in manner consistent with the other declared purposes of the Preamble—the "Union" will only be "more perfect." This, however, should come as no surprise because our experience with union of the kind and on the scale attempted by the Constitution had no parallel in our tradition. The Framers do not pretend to know, nor do they presume the people to know, what a "perfect Union" is, even though, we repeat, they seem to have a notion of what constitutes a "more perfect Union." In sum, we should expect, off a careful reading of the Preamble, that when speaking about the nature of the "Union" there still will exist room for honest controversy and debate that cannot be resolved satisfactorily through the forms and processes established by the Constitution.[4]

And what of the other purposes set forth in the Preamble, particularly justice? Are we to assume that justice could be

[4] In this connection the major works of John Marshall, Joseph Story, John Taylor, and John C. Calhoun come readily to mind.

defined in such an invariant fashion that disputes would not arise about its content and meaning? Not at all. We could reasonably infer that justice will be that which emerges from the system established by the Constitution. (This, of course, involves even further assumptions with which we will deal later.) The text of the Preamble reads to this effect: "We the People of the United States, in Order to . . . establish Justice . . . do ordain and establish this Constitution. . . ." This language stands in sharp contrast to that of the Declaration as interpreted by the high priests of the official literature. We can easily illustrate this: To say that "We the People" do ordain and establish" a government "in Order to" promote desired ends is quite different from saying, as does the Declaration, that "Governments are instituted among Men" to secure certain "rights." The words of the Preamble tell us that men, "We the People," are instituting government in order to promote purposes or ends to which "We the People" subscribe. And by implication, at least, the Preamble suggests that this entire process is not predestined: Rather it is a matter of deliberate choice, so much so that the people can and have a "right" to establish their own ends or purposes when constituting a government, not ends derived from a source other than the people. This does not mean the Framers did not envision dispute over the meaning of or the priority of the ends. If this were the case, they would have had little reason to write the remainder of the document, which in effect sets forth the procedures by which we are to fulfill the ends of the Preamble. The presumption is clearly that the people operating under the forms and processes established by the Constitution can conscientiously subscribe to the proposition that justice will be forthcoming.

(d) As we have noted (and our experience indicates that this fact comes as something of a surprise to many undergraduates) , there is no mention of equality in the Preamble. What are we to make of this? How can it be that in the very Preamble which does constitute us as a nation, there is no mention of that which Lincoln and the official literature inform us is our overriding commitment, or that to which we are presumably dedicated as a people. This is serious business because, if we accept the Lincolnian interpretation of our tradition and its supreme commitment, the very symbol of equality vanishes in a period of approximately thirteen years. Surely, the Preamble of the Constitution would be the very place to re-emphasize our commitment to equality if, indeed, equality were taken to be our supreme commitment. Its omission, therefore, can hardly be considered a matter of simple oversight.

This is such a sensitive point (even though it is not set forth in the terms we have employed) that we find, and not without good reason, explanations offered for this turn of events in the official literature. The most popular explanation runs as follows: Between the times of the Declaration and the Constitution, the more "conservative" elements of the country gained control and put the brakes on the "liberal" ideals of the Revolution.[5] Such an explanation comes as no surprise, especially from those who would prefer the Lincolnian interpretation of our tradition, but the evidence for such a contention is very flimsy. Usually much is made of the fact that Patrick Henry, a staunch advocate of separation, could not bring himself to support the Constitution. Or, in a more general vein, some contend that the "cast of characters" did change from the time of the Declaration and the adoption of the Constitution; that is, relatively few who subscribed to the Declaration signed the Constitution. To answer such a contention would consume time better spent on other enterprises. However, we can say this much: First, we should expect the "cast" to change after a period of thirteen years. The experi-

5 James Allen Smith was one of the first to dwell on this point.

ences of our lifetime should tell us as much and countless examples could be offered. Second, individuals with sharply divergent views—*e.g.*, Paine, Adams, Jefferson, and Hamilton —have very kind words to say about the Constitution and they did not perceive a shift of the kind and degree maintained by many of our more contemporary intellectuals. In fact, the view that somehow we, as a people, "veered off course" is a fabrication invented by those who like us to believe that the Declaration does represent our tradition and that we have to invent excuses for the fact that we have not subsequently behaved as if the Declaration were an "act of founding." It is a fabrication, we can say, fed by the Lincoln heresies, which only gained acceptance and legitimacy in our academic circles shortly after the turn of the century.[6]

One other point of some importance, and we shall be done with these contentions which suggest that the Constitution represents something resembling a betrayal of our tradition —that is, the tradition presumably embodied in the "all men are created equal" clause of the Declaration. Those who hold this view should have little use for any argument such as that set forth above. Even granting, *arguendo*, that (*a*) the Declaration can be accorded constitutional status and (*b*) the "all men are created equal" clause contains within it our supreme symbol—that is, our overriding commitment as a people interpreted in the broadest sense—we must still ask: Does the Declaration, in light of the Preamble, still obligate us? The answer, to the extent that we use the theory of the consent— which we assume must underlie Lincoln's contentions in the Gettysburg address—is "no" on two very valid counts: (*a*) The Constitution, a document which does enjoy constitutional status, gives us new commitments, new purposes, new symbols,

6 A brilliant answer to most of these contentions is to be found in John Roche's article "The Founding Fathers: A Reform Caucus in Action," *American Political Science Review* (March, 1962) .

and equality, however defined, is not one of them. (*b*) Precisely to the extent we acknowledge that the Framers were, so to speak, "backing off" from the symbols or symbol of the Declaration (in the sense we have indicated above) , we have every reason to believe that they wanted to let us "off the hook" or, more bluntly, to indicate clearly that equality is no longer one of our basic commitments.

The remainder of the Constitution is devoted, in large part, to the establishment of mechanisms and procedures through which "We the People" are to fulfill the purposes of the Preamble. And, as we have said, the main features of the Constitution and the theory underlying it are best understood in light of the teaching of *The Federalist,* wherein we find the supreme symbols of the American tradition, rule by the deliberate sense of a virtuous people, held up to us.

We can best approach *The Federalist* and its central teaching by taking up the contentions advanced in the official literature which run something as follows: "Yes, the Framers do talk of 'We the People' in the Preamble but surely they could not have meant this in light of the structure and procedures they subsequently set forth in the body of the Constitution, some of which are clearly designed to prevent rule by the people. Look at the bicameral legislature with the standard for representation of one of the chambers based (irrevocably) on the principle of state equality. Or look at the mode of election they provided for the election of Presidents. What is worse, if we take Publius at his word, the Constitution was never really intended to allow 'We the People' to rule. In the Tenth *Federalist* Publius informs us, in a roundabout fashion, that the very nature of the Union, quite apart from the structure and procedures of government, is such that the people (the major part of them) cannot rule." [7]

[7] See, for one example, James McGregor Burns, *Deadlock of Democracy* (Englewood Cliffs, N.J.: Prentice-Hall, Inc., 1963) .

Such contentions involve a number of considerations which we will try to disentangle as best we can. A good point of departure seems to be Federalist 10, because it is conceded on all sides to be the single most important statement we have concerning the theoretical underpinnings of our constitutional system. Let us briefly present those aspects of Publius' argument that are usually seized upon by the custodians of the lore to bolster their arguments concerning the "undemocratic" character of our system.

First, according to Publius, there are very grave dangers associated with "popular government" or rule, we may take it, by "We the People." Societies—and here we paraphrase Publius—have a distinct propensity to break up into factions. Factions, either majority or minority, are, according to Publius, "united and actuated by some common impulse of passion, or of interest, adverse to the rights of other citizens, or to the permanent and aggregate interests of the community." Publius also tells us that it would be undesirable to eliminate factions because this would involve a stringent curtailment of liberty and even beyond this, factions probably cannot be eliminated even if we try our best. His very words are: "The latent causes of faction are . . . sown in the nature of man." However, relief from factions can be had "by controlling [their] effects." And here we come across a very interesting passage: "If a faction consists of less than a majority, relief is supplied by the republican principle, which enables the majority to defeat its sinister views by regular vote. It may clog the administration, it may convulse the society; but it will be unable to execute and mask its violence under the forms of the Constitution." What Publius is telling us in no uncertain terms is that our system, operating under republican principles, does not have a great deal to fear from minority factions —these factions will be quashed by the majority. This passage represents the first and last we are to hear about minority factions and, we may safely assume, this problem certainly was not uppermost in his mind.

The hard question—and Publius does face it head on—is: What about majority factions? Is it at all possible, consistent with republican principles, to control their effects? The bulk of this essay is devoted to answering these and related questions. The general answers to these questions take this form: "Either the existence of the same passion or interest in a majority at the same time must be prevented, or the majority, having such co-existent passion or interest, must be rendered, by their number and local situation, unable to concert and carry into effect schemes of oppression." While Publius holds out little hope that either of the conditions can be obtained in a "democracy," by which he means "direct democracy" wherein decisions are made directly by the people meeting together for this very purpose, he does see great hope for fulfilling them in the United States. Here we come upon one of Publius' central teachings: Because the United States is extensive in both size and population there is need for a representative system of government. The mere necessity for representation helps insure that factious majorities will not be able to impose their will. Why so? Because in a republic (= representative democracy) the "public views" will be refined and enlarged through a "chosen body of citizens, whose wisdom may best discern the true interest of their country, and whose patriotism and love of justice will be least likely to sacrifice it to temporary or partial considerations." Moreover, as the republic grows, the number of fit individuals compared with the number of available seats in Congress will also grow by leaps and bounds so that the citizens will have ample opportunity to fix their attention on those men "who possess the most attractive merit, and the most diffusive and established characters." Beyond this, the very size of the country coupled with the availability of meritorious candidates will make it "more difficult for unworthy candidates to practise with success the vicious arts, by which elections are too often carried."

Another concomitant of extensiveness, and a matter which has received the most attention in our literature, is, in Publius' words, this: "Extend the sphere, and you take in a greater variety of parties and interests; you make it less probable that a majority of the whole will have a common motive to invade the rights of other citizens; or if such a common motive exists, it will be more difficult for all who feel it to discover their own strength, and to act in unison with each other." According to this reasoning, a faction might be able to temporarily get its way in, say, a state or portion thereof, but the chances of its imposing its will on the entire country are remote.

There is a great deal more in Federalist 10, but we will stop here because we have before us sufficient information to understand those charges frequently made in the official literature concerning Publius' answer to the problem of majority factions. Their contentions come to something like this: "Only superficially do you (Publius) appear to answer the question to which you addressed yourself. If, as you say, an extended republic, by the very nature of its extensiveness, presents inherent barriers to rule by majority factions, then, why don't these same barriers also operate to prevent the formation of non-factious majorities? Why is it—and this you seem to gratuitously assume—that only factious majorities will be stymied by those factors associated with our extensiveness? Why not as well majorities intent upon promoting justice, the general welfare, and other purposes stated in the Preamble?"

These are good questions, which take on even greater force if we recall Publius' argument that majorities will be able to operate in our system to prevent minority factions from having their way. We are, indeed, faced with something of a puzzle—we shall call it the "filter puzzle"—because, on the one hand, we are told that non-factious, anti-factious, and, certainly we must assume, virtuous majorities will be able to rule, while factious majorities will find the obstacles associated with the extensiveness of the republic too much of an obstacle to overcome. Put otherwise, and this is why we dub it the filter puzzle, the "bad" or factious majorities will be somehow "filtered" out because of those factors associated with extensiveness.

Some students of the American political system have in recent years suggested that the filter problem is insoluble or, more accurately, incapable of resolution off of *The Federalist*.[8] Explanations touching upon the question of what Publius was really "up to" abound, most of them uncharitable. Probably the most common is that Publius really wanted an inert government—one, that is, that would be relatively inactive and certainly one that would be non-responsive to any popular will, factious or not. More: As some contend, he viewed the Constitution as a means to protect intrenched interests, particularly the well-to-do.[9] Any such explanations, however, certainly fail to take into account the rather obvious fact that one of the paramount objectives of the Philadelphia Convention was to establish a more vigorous and powerful government. Moreover, the line of reasoning used in Federalist 10 does not permit of any analysis of what Publius "wanted" or what the Framers "wished." Those factors cited for the difficulties factious majorities will encounter are concomitants of the extensiveness of the republic; they are "givens" and in no way the handiwork of man any more than the earth's rotation. The barriers to the formation of factious majorities are, as the text makes abundantly clear, what we today fashionably call "in-

8 See Robert Dahl's *Preface to Democratic Theory* (Chicago: University of Chicago Press, 1956).

9 For Charles Beard's thesis, see *An Economic Interpretation of the Constitution of the United States* (New York: Macmillan Company, 1913). For a different view of the matter see Robert E. Brown, *Charles Beard and the Constitution* (Princeton: Princeton University Press, 1956).

formal," "social," or "environmental" in nature, as distinct from "formal" or "structural" which suggest conscious man-made design.

Other critics tend to the position that Publius was unaware of the "inconsistency" of his argument or, if he was, he wanted to skirt the issue so as not to rock the boat at a very critical point in the ratification process, since any "solution" would not be in keeping with the "republican principle" presumably embodied in our Constitution. This latter explanation in one way or another also takes us back to the assumption that the Framers, and Publius in particular, though speaking the vocabularly of republicanism, really wanted some kind of minority control.

Now these "charges" against Publius are very serious and we must ask ourselves: Is there any way we can render Publius consistent? Is there any means by which, consistent with his professed principles and more general theory, we can "solve" the filter puzzle? In our view there is, and the solution takes the following form:

Publius is telling us in this essay—and others as well—that the process of majority formation in the United States will be difficult, equally for factious and non-factious majorities. Programs and proposals that are advanced will be scrutinized and debated at length and, beyond this, we have reason to believe off of Publius' teachings, they will engender a certain suspicion among representatives and ordinary citizens alike. Only on the most extraordinary occasions, such as an external attack upon the country, can we expect the majority-will to make itself felt without delay of some sort—a delay which is a necessary concomitant of our extensiveness. All this seems obvious enough but we are still left to wonder what this delay has to do with the filtering process. This we can answer as follows: Delay is requisite for, or, in other words, allows for, the emergence of a consensus among the people concerning proposals and programs in the political arena—a consensus that is, in important particulars, different from just simple majority rule which characterizes direct democracy. In the very process of discussion and debate both individuals and groups will not only be heard—particularly as proposals for action do affect them or seek to regulate their way of life—but also to suggest modifications and strike "deals" that render such programs more palatable to a greater number within society. Put another way, delay provides the opportunity for "give and take"— for that kind of subtle process which characterizes humane societies to take place, wherein binding decisions are taken only after opinions are allowed to settle on the available alternatives, and this only after due account has been made for the arguments pro and con with an eye to the sentiments, feelings, and probable reaction of those whose cooperation is essential for the successful implementation of the policy or program under discussion.[10] Now, to be sure, Publius does not speak precisely in this language or in these terms. Nevertheless, we do not strain the text or the central tenets of his teachings when we say that he must have something very akin to consensual politics in mind. His animus towards a plebiscitary system coupled with his emphasis upon the advantages and virtues associated with an extended republic certainly seems to make this clear. And even our contemporary adverse critics of Publius grant that he placed great emphasis upon the construction of a consensual system. Moreover, as these critics are quick to inform us, the development of our institutions and procedures after our founding (especially congressional procedures and political parties) have proceeded in a manner fully consonant with Publius' grand design.

We are now prepared to ask the central question: Why should delay, even granting it contributes to the development

10 See Kendall and Carey, "The Intensity Problem and Democratic Theory," *American Political Science Review* (March, 1968) .

and perpetuation of consensual politics, serve to filter our majority factions while, simultaneously, responding to the wishes of non-factious majorities? At one level, the answer seems obvious: The possibilities of hasty, ill-considered, intemperate, and rash action are considerably reduced. The mere extensiveness of the republic "forces" us as a people or nation to heed the very advice that we would probably give a friend who, in a moment of passion, seems intent upon doing something we are sure he will later live to regret, namely, cool off, calm down, reflect about the situation at hand before acting. But this is only one part of the answer. Delay and deliberation do not inherently prevent rule by factions, either majority or minority. Those bent upon committing the most monstrous crimes against society (as the Nazis and Communists have been known to do) also deliberate, plan, and calculate. Delay, deliberation, consensus, all taken together, by no means insure against tyranny or control by factions. Publius' belief that these factors would serve to block factious majorities is clearly based on two related assumptions—assumptions which are not articulated in Federalist 10 but which are nevertheless there and serve to give meaning to *The Federalist*. We can put them as follows: (*a*) The American people, unlike perhaps other people, have a sense of right and wrong; they do have, in other words, a feeling for justice and doing that which promotes the true interests of the community. (*b*) Off at the end, if given sufficient opportunity (which involves time to deliberate and meditate), the vast majority of the American people will opt for that which is just and designed to promote the permanent and aggregate interests of the community; they will, to turn the proposition around, reject the appeals of factions. And with this we have come back to the supreme symbols of the American tradition, that is, to the symbols of a virtuous people through deliberative processes striving to achieve and advance their declared purposes which involve, *inter alia,* better ordering with justice.

Other essays in *The Federalist* indicate quite clearly that Publius is falling back upon our supreme and oldest symbols. In Federalist 51, the latter part of which is a rehash of the arguments presented in Federalist 10, Publius rejects outright the very notion that we must recur to "a will in the community independent of the majority" either for the protection of the "rights of the minority" or the pursuit of justice.[11] In this connection we also find this statement: "In the extended republic of the United States, and among the great variety of interests, parties, and sects which it embraces, a coalition of a majority of the whole society could seldom take place on any other principles than those of justice and the general good." Or, going to Federalist 63, speaking in the context of the functions to be performed by the Senate, Publius writes:

As the cool and deliberate sense of the community ought in all governments, and actually will in all free governments ultimately prevail over the view of its rulers; so there are particular moments in public affairs when the people stimulated by some irregular passion, or some illicit advantage, or misled by artful misrepresentations of interested men, may call for measures which they themselves will afterwards be the most ready to lament and condemn. In these critical moments, how salutary will be the interference of some temperate and respectable body of citizens, in order to check the misguided career, and to suspend the blow meditated by the people against themselves, until reason, justice and truth, can regain their authority over the public mind?

Other illustrations of this nature abound in the text.

---

11 Publius' rejection was unlike, we might add, some of our contemporary libertarians who seem to have a penchant to appeal to some source almost totally independent of the community (*e.g.,* the Supreme Court) for resolution of some of our most perplexing social problems.

The assumptions we have set forth do render Publius a consistant political theorist on the very points he is accused of gross theoretical inconsistency by the official literature. In light of this, two interesting questions are: Why does the official literature overlook or ignore those assumptions which are plainly warranted from both the text and our traditional symbols? Why is it that the official custodians of the lore have not sought to provide those assumptions which would render Publius' theory meaningful and free from those seeming contradictions which render *The Federalist* rather meaningless, even susceptible to the accusation of being nothing more than deceitful propaganda, and, most certainly, a document illdeserving of our serious attention for an understanding of the tradition and our Constitution?

The answer, we submit, resides ultimately in the fact that the official literature looks to the Declaration as somehow marking our beginnings and providing us with our supreme symbols and commitments as a people. Little wonder, from what we have said in the previous chapters, that the official literature cannot place the Declaration in its proper context; little wonder that it exhibits a total ignorance of the tradition that both preceded and followed the Declaration; and, finally, little wonder, given the emphasis placed upon the equality symbol wrenched from the context of the Declaration, that it seeks to "prove" the Constitution and *The Federalist* do not really "fit" within our tradition. In short, to view the Declaration as the official custodians do, precludes even an awareness, much less an understanding, of the basic assumptions underlying Publius' theory.

Two other matters of considerable importance treated in *The Federalist* are also best understood in light of the basic assumptions that we have set forth. We will treat them only briefly. First, there is the matter of "separation of powers" which involves a division of governing authority among the three branches of government established by the Constitution. Second, there is also a division of function and authority between the national and state governments which we refer to today as "federalist." Let us take up these matters.

(*a*) The Constitution represents an attempt at a union of sovereignties on a scale previously unknown. One whose theoretical "weather eye" is peeled can see at once that this is a most difficult situation which in due course is going to lead to controversy necessitating differentiation of existing symbols in a radically different context than that known to those who drafted the Constitution. In other words, we as a people are not quite sure in this new setting precisely how we are to organize ourselves for action in history. For this reason, we should not at all be surprised that controversies surrounding state-national relations were very much at the fore at the time of ratification. Nor should we be surprised that they are still very much with us.

Only at one level does *The Federalist* answer those questions concerning the nation and its component parts. The answer, as we might expect, is procedural in nature and once again brings into play the deliberate sense of the community. "If ... the people should in future become more partial to the federal than to the State governments, the change can only result from such manifest and irresistible proofs of better administration. ... And in that case, the people ought not surely to be precluded from giving most of their confidence where they may discover it to be most due." [12] Or, from the same paper and on the very same subject: "The ultimate authority [regarding state-national jurisdiction in the case of conflicts] wherever the derivative may be found, resides in the people alone; and that it will not depend merely on the comparative ambition or address of the different governments, whether

[12] From Federalist 46.

either, or which of them, will be able to enlarge its sphere of
jurisdiction at the expense of the other. Truth no less than de-
cency requires, that the event in every case, should be supposed
to depend on the sentiments and sanction of their common
constituents." Such an answer to this very perplexing problem
comes as no surprise given the underlying assumptions of *The
Federalist*.

(*b*) Separation of powers presents us with problems of a
slightly different order. Here we shall only discuss one aspect
of it that bears upon Publius' commitment to deliberate rule
by the people. This, partly for reasons we have spelled out,
cannot, according to Publius, be achieved if there is accumula-
tion of all powers (judicial, legislative, and executive) of government in the hands of the one, the few, or the many.[13] The
evident fear, for reasons that are not entirely spelled out by
Publius, is that the governors or those in control of the powers
would in the absence of separation of powers possess something akin to an irresistible temptation to tyrannize the people.

However, the major problems associated with our system of
separation of powers have, over the decades, come to something like the following: Each of the branches could, if they
were to use the constitutional powers at their disposal, conceivably bring the entire national government to a standstill.
Or, to approach this from another angle, Who is to decide
among the branches when there is a "falling out" among them
concerning the extent of their constitutional powers relative
to one another or to the people? We could easily imagine,
granting that the three departments are "equal and coordinate," that the "gears" of our system might well "lock" in such
circumstances.

The Constitution provides only an indirect answer to those

13 See Federalist 47. This view was shared by almost every major figure at
the time of founding.

problems relating to the relationship between the branches. And this answer is not the one we are given in most of our contemporary texts which seem to grant the Supreme Court the special prerogative to authoritatively handle such questions. Consistent with the "We the People" of the Preamble, the body of the Constitution does vest the "final say" in Congress provided sufficient majorities can be mustered. Congress through the impeachment processes can remove the President and justices of the Court, whereas there is nothing the President or Court can do, no matter how intensely they feel, to Congress. There is also, at another level, provision for resolution of conflicts of this nature through the amendment process in which neither the President nor the Court, formally speaking, participate.

To all of this we hasten to add the following: The "weapons" at the disposal of Congress or Congress and the state legislatures were obviously intended, given the constitutional morality set forth by Publius, to be used only in the most extreme cases, not for "light and transient causes." The very protection provided the Executive and the Court against Congress acting in an arbitrary manner (*e.g.*, the extra majorities required for removal from office through the impeachment process) are testimony of this. Publius goes beyond this: We are duly informed in more places than one that the legislature is most likely to attempt to draw all powers unto itself, and the need for protection must be provided the executive and judiciary.

But, in noting this, we should not "take our eye off the ball" and overlook what certainly is the core of Publius' teachings. We can say with certainty that he did not anticipate constitutional crises of this kind arising save upon the most extraordinary occasions. To believe otherwise would be tantamount to admitting that the Philadelphia Constitution would be next to inoperable and hence totally incapable of fulfilling the purposes of government set forth in the Preamble. His teachings clearly urge a cooperation among the branches. So much is clear from Publius' repudiation of the doctrine that the branches should be completely separated from one another or, as Publius puts it, the doctrine of separation of powers does not mean that the "departments ought to have no *partial agency* in, or no control over, the acts of each other." [14] Yet there is another side to this interdependence which involves a healthy sense of self-restraint on the part of the departments. Lacking self-restraint (something which is actually imposed upon the Congress through express consitutional provision), the very cooperation necessary for the operation of government is endangered. In a war of "all against all" among our branches, the Senate, for example, might refuse to cooperate with a President who has shown lack of self-restraint in his dealings with the legislative branch. The Congress might well decide to take drastic action against a Supreme Court that overtly challenges the authority of Congress. We can well imagine any number of conflicts that might occur to bring our system to the very brink of a total breakdown.

The self-restraint and cooperation of which we speak is in a very real sense much akin to the consensual politics to which we have referred. And we should not be surprised that until the time of the Civil War the morality urged upon us by Publius was adhered to, judging from the number of times the President and the Court used their ultimate weapons with respect to the will of the people as interpreted by Congress. Since that time, however, we seem, as even the official literature informs us, to have run into great difficulties. The reasons for our difficulties can also be traced to a derailment in our tradition, the causes of which we will explore further.

---

14 From Federalist 47.

CHAPTER VII

The Tradition and
the Bill of Rights

We can now analyze the so-called Bill of Rights, usually defined as the first ten amendments to our Constitution. The official literature, as we might well expect, has already taken great care to supply us with answers to most of those questions that arise concerning the Bill of Rights and its place in our tradition. Its teachings come down to something like this: The Declaration of Independence and the Bill of Rights, theoretically speaking, fit "hand in glove." More exactly, the Bill of Rights follows in the "spirit" of the Declaration by asserting individual rights that limit arbitrary and abusive action by government. It is worth our while to examine some of the contentions found in the official literature upon which such an estimate of the Bill of Rights seems to be based.

Contention One: The Bill of Rights was intended to correct an oversight of the Constitutional Convention. The fifty-five at Philadelphia somehow did not appreciate the extent to which the people wanted their basic rights enumerated in the Constitution. On this score, at least, they certainly were not attuned to the times or to the spirit of either the people or the revolution.

Whether the Framers were out-of-step with their times— which is one of the stock charges of those who claim the Declaration marks the origins of tradition this side of the Atlantic— is a question we shall leave open save to point out that this

119

seems not to be the case given the speed with which the Constitution was drafted and adopted. The "oversight" theory, however, falls flat on its face because of certain obvious facts. First, the matter of whether to include a Bill of Rights in the Constitution was brought up before the Philadelphia Convention and was rejected unanimously, each state voting as a unit. Second, we find the subject of a Bill of Rights discussed in Federalist 84, wherein the charge is made that the addition of a Bill of Rights would not only be unnecessary but dangerous —a matter we will go into at some length later. But we are hardly entitled off of the plain record to say that the omission of a Bill of Rights was an oversight. On the contrary, it was by all outward evidences deliberate.

Contention Two: The Constitution would not have been adopted unless the pro-Constitution forces promised that a Bill of Rights would be written into or added onto the Constitution.

Of all the fictions that have grown up around the Bill of Rights and the adoption of the Constitution, this is quite probably the most unbelievable. Who, we might ask, could make any such commitment? How could promises of such a nature be extracted from the pro-Constitution forces when the participants in the state ratifying conventions (all thirteen of them) had only to look at the document before them to see precisely what the amendment process entailed. Certainly no group in the ratification conventions was in any position to do more than say: "Yes, if we, or one of our members, is elected to the Congress, we pledge ourselves to bring the matter up. Moreover, we will, insofar as possible, try to secure passage of the desired amendment." But given the amendment process which calls for a two-thirds vote of both houses of Congress and a three-fourths approval of the states, they could not have *promised* anything beyond this. And the plain undisputed fact is that the Constitution was ratified without a Bill of Rights.

Contention Three: The Bill of Rights is closely linked to the Declaration of Independence because the Bill of Rights is couched in terms very much akin to the Declaration's. At least both documents speak of "rights" in the sense that there are things which no duly constituted government should do.

This is *at best* only partially true. The word "right" or "rights" appears six times in the Bill of Rights. Three times it is employed with respect to matters that relate principally to the administrative and judicial branches. "In all criminal prosecutions, the accused shall enjoy the right of a speedy and public trial . . . ." Or, "The right of the people to be secure in their persons, houses, papers, and effects, against unreasonable search and seizures, shall not be violated." The Ninth Amendment (which we will discuss later in a different context) contains the word "rights," and the Second Amendment speaks of "the right of the people to keep and bear Arms," [1] a right which, as we have recently been reminded by some of our intellectual leaders, is best forgotten if for no other reason than certain reasonable regulations are necessary to promote domestic tranquility. None of these rights is at all exceptional in the sense that they represent a departure from our tradition to the time of the Constitution. None of them (save possibly the Second Amendment) can impinge upon our basic commitment as a people since they are not directed as limitations on the people operating through their representative institutions to enact the deliberate will of the community. On the contrary, the administrative and judicial arms of government are, with the enactment of these amendments, bound by rules or modes of procedure which seem to be the product of a slow and deliberate evolution within our tradition. Most of the rights in the Bill of Rights—and we want to make this clear—bear no resemblance to the "unalienable rights" of the Decla-

1 Poore, I.

ration but rather to the "rights" that "We the People" have devolved upon for our better ordering—rights, that is to say, which are part and parcel of a tradition that has its origins well before the Declaration.

On top of this, the Bill of Rights does not mention "equality," much less even reaffirm in any fashion whatsoever that which the official literature claims to be our supreme commitment off of the Declaration. Nor can the rights set forth in the Bill of Rights be regarded as *unalienable*: they are rights that can be modified or even repudiated through the very same process by which they were adopted.

But let us leave the matter of contentions aside, for, as the reader will soon see, most of the claims of the official literature with respect to the Bill of Rights have no foundation in fact. In this regard, we can go so far as to say that contemporary libertarians, who comprise a pretty healthy majority of those who interpret and explain the American political tradition out across the nation in our institutions of higher learning, are guilty of attributing their values to those who were responsible for the adoption of the Bill of Rights.

To this point we have purposely ignored the First Amendment. We have done so because the First Amendment presents us with a very special problem that requires some intensive analysis (Amendments Two through Ten, so far as we can tell, do not).[2] The First Amendment provisions do apply to Congress and hence, indirectly, to the people, so that we are entitled to read the amendment as a limitation on the deliberate sense of the community. We can put the matter this way: If "We the People" are truly upset about what certain individuals and groups in society are saying or writing publicly, whether the speeches or writings urge revolution, simple

2 They do not because our tradition as far back as the Massachusetts Body of Liberties always placed great stress on preventing abuses by the executive and judicial arms of government.

disobedience to the laws, contain obscenities, or whatever, "We the People"—or so the amendment can be interpreted—have no legitimate authority to regulate or meddle with such writings or publications through national laws.[3] More precisely, any regulation through normal political channels (*i.e.*, through the law-making process as defined by the Constitution) would at least require the "repeal" of the First Amendment. It is a short step from this view to the proposition that the drafters of the First Amendment intended to commit us as a people irrevocably to what is now fashionably termed an "open society" which places an extremely high premium on the toleration of dissent. And from here it is even a shorter step to the proposition that the First Amendment, particularly the speech and press provisions, embodies the essence of the revolutionary ideals expressed in the Declaration.

Bearing this in mind let us turn to Federalist 84, wherein Publius does argue against a Bill of Rights in the sense it was contended for during the ratification struggle. The first thing we must note is that the word "right" in the common law tradition—and this tradition was still dominant at the time the Bill of Rights was drafted—confers a very special status upon that which is specified as a right. To label something, either of substantive or procedural nature, a right is tantamount to establishing a limitation on the powers of *governors* *against* the *people* or *individuals*. So much was true with respect to the Magna Carta, the Petition of Rights, and the Declaration of Rights in the English tradition. And this is precisely why Publius could argue when speaking of rights: "According to their primitive signification, they have no application to constitutions professedly founded upon the power

---

[3] Of course, with the broad interpretation given the Fourteenth Amendment by the Supreme Court, the same prohibitions now apply against the states. The Court's interpretation, we hasten to add, just "happens" to correspond with the philosophy of the official literature on these and like matters.

of the people, and executed by their immediate representatives and servants. Here, in strictness, the people surrender nothing, and as they retain everything, they have no need of particular reservations. 'WE, THE PEOPLE of the United States, to secure the blessings of liberty to ourselves and our posterity, do *ordain* and *establish* this Constitution for the United States of America.' " [4]

Publius' point is well taken. If—and this happens to be the case—we have been regarding rights in the context of limitations on the authority, then what sense does it make for the sovereign people to limit themselves? Surely, the security for any such rights of the people against the people must ultimately depend, as Publius tells us, "on the general spirit of the people and of the government." [5]

But Publius does talk about certain rights in a very favorable manner. He even goes so far as to declare that those rights contained in the Constitution (*i.e.*, prohibition against bills of attainder, ex post facto laws, guarantee of writ of habeas corpus and prohibition against titles of nobility) are "in every rational sense, and to every useful purpose, A BILL OF RIGHTS." Now we must ask, isn't Publius guilty of a gross inconsistency? He hails those rights already in the body of the Constitution but rather strongly opposes the addition of other rights—specifically "liberty of the press." If the specification of some rights is worthwhile and efficacious, why shouldn't a further elaboration of rights also serve a useful purpose? Publius' answer we briefly may put as follows:

(*a*) The national government is not intended to regulate "every species of personal and private concerns." Rather it is established with the intent "to regulate the general political interests of the nation." Thus, there is little need for detailed specification of personal liberties and rights. Moreover, Pub-

---

4 Cooke (ed) , *The Federalist*. Emphasis his.
5 Robert Dahl reminds us of this in his *Preface to Democratic Theory*.

lius intimates, the states should be charged with the task of any such detailed specification because the scope of their authority does involve personal and private concerns.[6]

(b) ". . . that bills of rights, in the sense and to the extent in which they are contended for, are not only unnecessary in the proposed constitution, but would even be dangerous." Why? They are unnecessary because the national government is a government of delegated powers and possesses no authority to infringe upon the rights which the opponents of the Constitution want to protect through amendments. "For why declare," Publius asks, "that things shall not be done which there is no power to do?" And, he declares, they would be dangerous for at least two reasons. First, "They would contain various exceptions to powers which are not granted; and, on this very account, would afford a colourable pretext to claim more than were granted." Second, to declare that government should not abuse a given right or liberty carries with it a presumption that the national government was originally vested with powers to regulate the rights and liberties in question. This affords those who are "disposed to usurp, a plausible pretence for claiming" that the national government still possesses, despite the bill of rights, the power to *properly* regulate the specified rights and liberties.

(c) There will be, Publius warns us, problems involved with the differentiation of rights such as liberty of the press. "What signifies," he asks, "a declaration that 'liberty of the press shall be inviolably preserved?' What is liberty of the press? Who can give it any definition which would not leave the utmost latitude for evasion?"

With this in mind we are in a position now to see why Publius supported the rights contained in the Constitution but rather vigorously opposed the inclusion or addition of other

---

[6] All of this represents a differentiation between society and government, a differentiation that is certainly not unexpected in light of our tradition.

rights "in the sense and to the extent in which they are contended for" such as liberty of the press. The rights which he does support, *i.e.*, those contained in the body of the Constitution, are (a) common-law rights as distinct from rights which are merely asserted by an individual or a group, (b) easily defined, in part because they are traditional and do not touch in any significant way upon the basic design of the Philadelphia Constitution. The "rights" he opposes (if we abstract from the one example he does offer, "liberty of the press") are susceptible of such a variety of definitions that they could subsequently be construed in such a fashion as to limit the legitimate exercise of delegated powers by the national government, to expand national powers at the expense of the states, or to limit severely the deliberate sense of the community operating through prescribed constitutional channels to handle those contingencies and conflicts that might in the future arise concerning the meaning and intent of the rights in question without having recourse to the amendment process. This latter point, often overlooked, surely must have been on his mind, for even the most important of the rights contained in the body of the Constitution, at least in Publius' estimation, the establishment of the writ of habeas corpus, can be suspended, presumably by Congress, "when in cases of rebellion or invasion the public safety requires it." We can understand, then, his reluctance, and even animus, towards the incorporation of less well-defined rights which could be construed so as to prevent resolution of future contingencies consonant with the purposes of the Preamble.

We see still another reason why, granting Publius' view of this matter, a wedge can be driven between the First Amendment of the Constitution and the other nine that comprise the Bill of Rights; why it is, as we have contended, that the First Amendment does deserve special attention. The "guts" of Amendments Two through Eight reassert well-established common-law rights about which there could scarcely be any controversy. The Ninth Amendment, of course, is an umbrella of sorts intended to answer counter-argument (*a*) above on Publius' part. And the Tenth is, as the Court aptly put it, nothing but a "truism" which simply reasserts Publius' view of the Constitution as expressed in Federalist 84 and elsewhere. Clearly, however, the First Amendment touches upon matters which Publius felt have no place in a bill of rights. From what we have said we can see reasons why he would be vigorously opposed to this amendment as it now stands, while still remaining rather indifferent about the other amendments which now constitute our Bill of Rights.

We can, without doing any injustice to Publius' arguments and the general thrust of his contentions, cast something of a different light on his arguments by asking: What is to prevent some individuals who subsequently become a majority in this nation from looking upon the First Amendment freedoms as providing us with a new commitment as a people organized for action in history? Would not a First Amendment containing these freedoms lead us to believe that we are committed to the precepts of an "open society"? Would not such contentions, in light of the Declaration and the interpretation given it in the official literature, make such good sense that subsequent generations might be disposed to believe our basic commitments are something other than those embodied in the Philadelphia Constitution and our prior tradition?

Publius, to be sure, does not provide us with direct answers to these questions. He was in a very poor position to envision the linkage that would be established in the minds of some between the Declaration and the freedoms which now constitute our First Amendment. Most surely he would have great difficulty in following the reasoning of those who contend in our day and age that the First Amendment embodies our supreme symbols. However, much to his credit, he did seem to sense that the specification of these and like freedoms could create very severe problems within our system.

Let us turn now to another episode regarding our Bill of Rights, the debates and proceedings of the first Congress which drafted and proposed them. In this we will see very few intimations that the Bill of Rights, and, in particular, the First Amendment freedoms of speech and press, represent any break with our tradition over the underlying principles of the Constitution.

Madison is frequently dubbed the "Father" of the Bill of Rights, as well he might be, given the seeming unflagging persistence he exhibited in the first Congress on behalf of their adoption. The House of Representatives, of which Madison was a member, was apparently very reluctant to take up the matter of a Bill of Rights. At least this much can be said, contrary to what is more or less accepted myth: The addition of a Bill of Rights was far from being the first concern of those who first met under the authority of the Constitution.[7]

Madison's speech of June 8, 1789, urging the adoption of a Bill of Rights, the longest and most detailed justification for the Bill of Rights we have in the official literature, hardly would lead one to believe that the Bill of Rights is the cornerstone of our republic. Nor, by all available evidence, did the first Congress which proposed it. To show this we need only point out the following which is a matter of official record:

(a) Madison's speech on behalf of the Bill of Rights is throughout conciliatory and moderate. The proposed amendments, he tells his audience, will not "endanger the beauty of Government [i.e., The Philadelphia Constitution] in any one important feature, even in the eyes of its most sanguine ad-

---

[7] Madison, as the record plainly shows, was rebuffed twice in his efforts to force this issue before the House. Even when he does gain the attention of the House there are those who still complain that there is more important business to attend to.

mirers." He is fully aware that some feel "paper barriers against the power of the community are too weak to be worthy of attention." But he counters: "As they have a tendency to impress some degree of respect for them, to establish the public opinion in their favor and rouse the attention of the whole community," they may still be of some merit. The argument he has heard to the effect that "by enumerating particular exceptions to the grant of power, it would disparage those rights which were not placed in that enumeration," he deems "the most plausible" objection to a Bill of Rights. But this he has "attempted" (and history, we add, has shown his attempt a dismal failure) to guard against by means of what subsequently turned out to be the Ninth Amendment.[8] [The final sentence of his address is probably the most revealing of his attitude toward the question of a Bill of Rights: "I have proposed nothing that does not appear to me as proper in itself, or eligible as patronized by a respectable number of our fellow-citizens; and if we can make the Constitution better in the opinion of those who opposed to it, without weakening its frame or abridging its usefulness in the judgment of those who are attached to it, we act the part of wise and liberal men to make such alterations as shall produce that effect." This "something to gain but nothing to lose" argument permeates most of his speech on behalf of the Bill of Rights, a fact which hardly supports the extravagant claims made for the Bill of Rights today] Moreover, we do not find, no matter how hard we search, that the House is under obligation to adopt a Bill of Rights because of promises made to the people. Nor do we

---

[8] The fact is that probably 99 percent of the American people cannot name a right provided by the Ninth Amendment. This, we can say, is an intriguing matter. It certainly tends to bear out a belief we have long held: You confer a very special status upon that which you formally declare as a right and, in so doing, tend to disparage those which, for one reason or another, are omitted. In any event, our contemporary "dialogue" illustrates this point, for we focus, when we do speak of rights, on those specified.

find the argument that the House is obliged to adopt the Bill
of Rights in response to overwhelming popular demand.

(b) The House of Representatives scarcely debates the
amendments submitted to it. Only eight individuals speak to
the proposal that "no religion shall be established by law,
nor shall the equal rights of conscience be infringed." The
House members spend even less time debating the proposed
amendment, "the Freedom of speech and of the press, and
the right of the people peaceably to assemble and consult for
their common good, and to apply to the Government for re-
dress of grievances, shall not be infringed." The fact is that
those proposals which subsequently were incorporated into
what is now the First Amendment, were not the subjects of
any extended or penetrating discussion. Those who lead us to
believe differently, and that would include certain members
of our Supreme Court who seem to speak with apodictic certainty about the intentions of the drafters of the First Amendment and other provisions of the Bill of Rights, can justly be
accused of not having done their homework. The debates in
the House tell us practically nothing about the matter of intent.

But this is significant in itself. The proposed amendments
were adopted by the House, some to be sure with modifications, in such a short period of time and with so little opposition that we have every reason to believe that they were taken
in the very spirit in which Madison first proposed them; namely, they would not in any way alter the basic structural or
procedural design of the Philadelphia Constitution. In other
words, every available bit of evidence would suggest that the
participants did not envision that the adoption of the amendments represented any departure from the basic principles
embodied in the Constitution. Yet this seems strange no matter how one looks at it. On the one hand, from the vantage
point of our contemporary intellectuals, duly echoed in num-

erous Supreme Court decisions, the drafters certainly must have meant to significantly modify, if not entirely change, the course of our tradition as expressed in the Constitution, at least to the extent of bringing it back into line with the "spirit" of the Declaration—at least as they interpret that "spirit." On the other, we should expect debate concerning the proposed amendments, principally those provisions which now constitute the First, because they are couched in such terms that we can easily envision their being interpreted in a fashion so as to significantly alter the fundamental nature of our Constitution and the government created by it. Indeed, we have today the benefit of hindsight but still we should expect that Madison's arguments might well have been challenged on the following grounds: "If we adopt these amendments we are severely circumscribing rule by 'We the People.' The 'listing' of rights in the manner you suggest is a highly presumptuous undertaking because such rights may very well be interpreted to deny future generations the flexibility and discretion to handle matters involving these very rights in a prudential manner consonant with the purposes of the Preamble." [9]

Two likely explanations for the behavior of the House suggest themselves. (a) The members of the House could have regarded the admonitions and prohibitions contained in the proposed Bill of Rights as nothing more than, to use John Marshall's words, "merely recommendatory." [10] Such a view, no matter how much at odds with our contemporary conception of the matter, is nevertheless quite plausible. We see this view expressed in Federalist 84, wherein we are so much as told that the rights contended for (and this certainly would

[9] Some indeed were prescient enough to see this. *Cf.* Charles Hyneman and George W. Carey (eds.), *A Second Federalist* (New York: Appleton, Century and Crofts, 1967), Chap. 2.

[10] Jonathan Elliot (ed.), *The Debates in the Several State Conventions on the Adoption of the Constitution* (Philadelphia, 1941, 2nd ed., rev.), III, 561.

include liberty of speech and press) "would sound much better in a treatise of ethics than in a constitution of government." And the salient parts of Madison's address suggest so much. For instance, the specification of rights he calls for in the form of amendments would "have a tendency to impress [upon the public or people] some degree of respect for them" and this "may be one means to control the majority from those acts to which they might be otherwise inclined."

[We can say with certainty, off of the state constitutions including even the Virginia Declaration of Rights, that those rights relating to our First Amendment freedoms were put in such terms as to be nothing more than prudent guides for public and legislative behavior.[11]]The same is true with respect to the "recommendatory amendments" submitted by the state constitutional ratifying conventions. For example, New York, one of four of the states which submitted the longest and most detailed amendment recommendations, proposed the following: "That the enjoyment of Life, Liberty, and pursuit of Happiness are essential rights which every Government *ought* to respect and preserve. . . ."[12] But note that the three other states (Rhode Island, North Carolina, and Virginia), by all evidences intent upon securing adoption of a bill of rights, employed the following language with respect to what is now part of our First Amendment "freedoms": "That the people have a right to freedom of speech, and of writing and publishing their sentiments; but the freedom of the press is one of the greatest bulwarks of liberty and *ought* not to be violated."[13]

Now note that the word "ought" is used with respect to the more sacred or fundamental "rights," whereas "shall," the

---

11 The following is taken from Charles Tansill (ed.), *Documents Illustrative of the Formation of the Union of the American States* (Washington: Government Printing Office, 1927).

12 Emphasis added.

13 *Ibid.*

mandatory form of expression, is employed with respect to lesser "rights." Much can be said about this rather curious wording (we say "curious" only in light of our contemporary interpretations of the meaning and intent of the Bill of Rights) but so much is clear: We can reasonably infer that the proposed amendments relating to speech and press were generally considered to be recommendatory—that is, of no legal binding or effect. This could well account for the absence of debate in the House, for it could well be that the proposed amendments, particularly as they relate to speech and press, were held to be something akin to New Year's resolutions.

(*b*) Considerable evidence can be mustered to show that those provisions relating to freedom of speech and press were to be understood and interpreted in the context of the existing common law of seditious libel which, for all intents and purposes, would serve to place regulation of these freedoms in the hands of the legislative assembly through the deliberative processes established by the Constitution. Harrison Gray Otis, speaking in the debates on the Alien and Sedition Acts, presents us with the accepted understanding of what the common law entailed: "This freedom [referring here to freedom of speech and press as contained in the First Amendment] is nothing more than the liberty of writing, publishing, and speaking one's thoughts, under the condition of being answerable to the injured party, whether it be the Government or an individual, for false, malicious, and seditious expressions, whether spoken or written; and the liberty of the press is merely an exemption from all previous restraints." [14] Clearly, then, if these freedoms were understood in the context of the common law of seditious libel, the Congress would still possess a considerable discretionary authority over their exercise—too much, at any rate, for our modern libertarians.

All available evidence, some of it admittedly indirect, leads

[14] See Hyneman and Carey, *A Second Federalist,* for our source.

us to believe that the provisions of the First Amendment relating to speech and press are best understood in the context of the common law. One important piece of indirect evidence is this: The select committee charged with winnowing through the proposals from the state ratifying conventions and drawing up amendment proposals for consideration by the House recommended that protection against infringement of speech and press also apply against state governments. The wording of their proposal is as follows: "No State shall infringe . . . the freedom of speech or of the press." We do know that in the vast majority of the states (probably ten of the eleven represented in the House) the common law of seditious libel was both accepted and in force. For this reason it is virtually impossible to believe that if this proposal were intended to eliminate the common law of seditious libel we would not find resistance and heated debate, particularly on the part of those who were a strong and vocal contingent in the House bent upon preserving the powers and autonomy of the states.[15]

Equally startling is this: There is virtually no debate about what freedom of speech and press would mean in the absence of the common law. Surely we should again expect extended debate if the traditional common-law standards were to be superseded. To assume that the members of the House knew precisely what these freedoms entailed in the absence of the common law would seem preposterous in light of the subsequent controversies surrounding these freedoms.

A relevant question with respect to the First Amendment as adopted, since it applies only to Congress, is this: Did the participants assume a federal or national law of seditious libel to exist? The bulk of the evidence would suggest that this was the case. Indeed, one sees off of Federalist 84 this very presumption. Moreover, as we have indicated, the fact that the

15 Leonard W. Levy, *Legacy of Suppression* (Cambridge: Harvard University Press, 1960).

prohibitions against the state and national governments were lumped together in the original proposal would clearly suggest that any intended restrictions were to apply equally to both levels of government. But again the absence of debate is revealing, for the participants certainly acted *as if* the provisions against the national government were no more severe than those against the state governments. This behavior is best explained on the assumption that prohibitions against the state and national governments were felt to be of the same order and to be interpreted in the same context, namely, that of the common law, Otherwise, if the prohibitions were not intended to apply equally in the same context—or if there were the slightest doubt about the matter—we should expect to find extensive and intensive debate about the proposal.

To this we may add the following. The participants certainly lacked any great corpus of literature on behalf of the libertarian ethic. To say that the members of the first Congress were captivated by those thoughts which charm our contemporary intellectuals concerning freedom is a proposition that will not withstand the most superficial critical examination. More: Madison, the "Father" of the Bill of Rights, tells us more than once in his public utterances on this question that the basic design of our system will not be altered by their adoption. Yet today we know that these Amendments, particularly the First, are interpreted to embody within them very drastic changes for the central symbol of our tradition, rule by the deliberate sense of the community. And we must ask, Could not the framers of these amendments see the potentialities inherent within them for altering the course of the American tradition? We must answer, Apparently not. As Aedanus Burke, a representative who very much wanted to change our direction as a nation, put the matter: "I am very well satisfied that those amendments that are reported and likely to be adopted by this House are very far from giving sat-

136

isfaction to our constituents; they are not those solid and substantial amendments which the people expect; they are little better than whip-syllabub, frothy and full of wind, formed only to please the palate; or they are like a tub thrown out to a whale, to secure the freight of the ship and its peaceable voyage." This, off of the available records, was the view of those of a substantial majority who voted for the proposed amendments.[16]

We can only conclude as follows concerning the Bill of Rights and the First Amendment: Their adoption did not alter the mainstream of the American tradition which, as the Preamble and *The Federalist* would have it, comes down to rule by the deliberate sense of the community. The Bill of Rights, contrary to what we have over the years been led to believe, did not constitute any departure from the tradition. Yes, indeed, our tradition was derailed and, to be sure, the Bill of Rights plays a critical role (because of deliberate distortion) in justifying the theories of those who support that derailment. But the real source of the derailment is not to be found in the Bill of Rights. It occurs, as best we can tell, at a point somewhat later in our history.

16 Paradoxically—paradoxical because it does conflict with the myth handed down to us by the official literature—the Antifederalists were not the champions of "civil liberties" (as we currently understand that term). They wanted to preserve the sovereignty of states vis-á-vis the national government. The record is abundantly clear on this point.

CHAPTER VIII

Derailment and the Modern Crisis

We have in the foregoing pages talked about a "derailment" in our tradition. The derailment, as we have further remarked, has understandably caused a certain schizophrenia among us, We the People, so that we do not really know who we are and where we are going. To detail when all this came to pass is far beyond our purpose here. We can, however, say this much: The philosophical plants of derailment were seeded and began to grow full force sometime between the very early years of the Republic and the Civil War. This is precisely why Lincoln could speak in the manner he did at Gettysburg and get away with it. These plants were lavishly fed and nourished, sometimes unwittingly, after the Civil War, so that by the turn of the century the so-called progressivist historians and political scientists could burst forth with their notions about the central symbols of the American tradition. In the intellectual world their interpretations have subsequently enjoyed remarkable and frightening success. Today, by and large, in the average college classrooms across the nation, it is their recounting of the American tradition and symbols (the Declaration of Independence and the Bill of Rights being their major sources) that is accepted pretty much as gospel truth, if we judge only by the texts that are most commonly used. Why two or more generations of presumed scholars fell under the spell of the "progressivists" is an intriguing matter.

Perhaps this question can be answered once we discover precisely why it is that the academic community is so philosophically out of step with the more general community of which it is presumably a part.

We can speak with a greater degree of certainty about the extent and causes of our derailment. Throughout, from our analysis of the Mayflower Compact to the Bill of Rights, we have emphasized that our supreme commitment and symbol has been self-government by a virtuous people. As we hope to have shown, the notion of legislative supremacy has been intimately linked with this symbol. We have, beyond any doubt, come a long way from any such self-interpretation. To show just how far we have come we need only reproduce a line of argument against our thesis well within the grasp of intelligent sophomores in our institutions of higher learning and most surely their instructors. One superficial but revealing manifestation of the derailment runs pretty much as follows:

"You have told us that there is a continuity from the Mayflower Compact through even the Bill of Rights. By this we understand you to mean that our Constitution is a legislative supremacy document, which leaves the Congress free to do, without let or hindrance, pretty much anything and everything it chooses to do. But all of this is surely not true. Ours is, if anything, a constitution of judicial supremacy. We do not, we in America, think of Congress as having the last word about its own powers, and what is more, Congress does not think of *itself* as having the last word. We have been taught that our Constitution is built on the principle of balance of powers specifically designed to prevent Congress *from* being supreme. We have in America three nominally equal and coordinate branches, legislative, executive, and judicial, each with power to check and balance the other, none of them therefore supreme in constitutional theory, none of them possessing the last say as a matter of constitutional theory, although in practice one of them does end up having the last say, namely, the Supreme Court. The Supreme Court, after all is said and done, finds itself called upon, year in and year out, to decide whether this or that act of Congress or of the President is or is not constitutional. In practice, it would seem, neither Congress nor the President ever talks back to the Supreme Court (very rarely, in any case), so that both of these branches are very much in the habit of accepting Supreme Court decisions. Beyond this, the Court must be supreme among the branches of government because the Constitution is supreme, and it is within the province of the Court to tell us what the Constitution means. Congress cannot exceed the powers expressly delegated to it in the Constitution, and Congress cannot invade the individual rights enthroned in the Bill of Rights, because if and when it were to try to the Supreme Court would, legitimately, bring it to heel."

This is a sensible objection to our thesis, and we hope to have stated it accurately and unprejudicially. We do recognize that it might be stated differently with a considerable amount of evidence to show its validity.[1] How, then, are we to answer?

Part of our answer would take this form: The plain language of the Constitution tells us unambiguously that Congress (whether the Congressmen think so or not is irrelevant) *is* supreme, and just can't help being supreme because the Constitution places in its hands weapons with which, when and if it chooses to use them, it can completely dominate the other two branches. If the Supreme Court says that such and such an act of Congress is null and void, Congress can, to begin with, reenact the statute and at the same time remove it from the jurisdiction of the Supreme Court. Or, it can reach for another weapon, more readily available if it has the President on its side: It can "pack" the Supreme Court. Or, it could

---

[1] The deans of our most prestigious law schools are wont to remind us of this periodically.

reach for still another weapon and remove justices through the impeachment process. Still another weapon is this: Congress could refuse to appropriate money for the Supreme Court justices in hopes of "starving" them into submission. And this, whatever one thinks about the morality of any of these weapons, is what the Constitution allows. There is no escaping this fact.

We know as well as anyone else that Congress does not in fact pack the Court, or impeach Supreme Court justices, or cut off their pay every time the Supreme Court challenges its authority; and only very rarely does it remove statutes from the Supreme Court's jurisdiction. In the vast majority of cases, when the Supreme Court does declare a statute of Congress unconstitutional, Congress, by long-standing habit, swallows hard and lets the Supreme Court (but notice we say *lets*) have its way—not, we imagine, because it has forgotten it has the ultimate weapons in its hand, and not necessarily because it in fact regards the Supreme Court's opinion as to what is constitutional and what isn't as better, wiser, or more inspired than its own. Why, then, does it allow the Supreme Court to have its way? *This, we submit, is a real mystery of our political system that for some strange reason the intellectual community has never chosen to recognize as a mystery. And, we say, the fact that it is not regarded as a mystery is indicative of how far our tradition has been derailed.*

Now let us try to clear up the mystery at, again, a fairly superficial level. First, unless Congress deems the issue at stake to be a very urgent one, it can lean back and let something called time take care of the matter. To put this rather bluntly, the mortality rate among Supreme Court justices happens to be very high; therefore we know that, at any given point in history, the dominant majorities or coalitions of the Court will not last for very long, and the President (if Congress indeed had the country on its side) will have named new justices who agree with Congress about what is constitutional. Congress, again presuming the country on its side, can clearly afford to play a game in which it cannot lose because the cards are stacked in its favor.

Second, just as Congress knows it has the ultimate weapons in its hands, the Supreme Court also knows that Congress, in case of a showdown, would win. The Supreme Court, therefore, may sometimes tailor its decisions a little, in order not to confront Congress with the temptation to bring the ultimate weapons to bear. Or, if that seems to be too strong a statement, we can at least say that considerations of prudence, particularly the consideration that you don't get yourself into a fight that you are sure to lose, might well dispose the Supreme Court to hold back any decision that might break the peace.

We have before us, then, two important facts which help to clear up the mystery. But the mystery still remains if Congress, as by all evidence it sometimes does, lets the Supreme Court have its way even when the statute in question *is* an urgent one. If, then, we are going to clear up the mystery we must come up with something better than the two reasons we have just named. And we believe the mystery can be resolved if we recall that for most purposes we in America do not live under the Philadelphia Constitution, or under the Bill of Rights, but under what we may term the "Federalist Papers Constitution." The "Federalist Papers," which we are in the habit of reading wrongly as an *explication* of the Constitution, in fact give us a new and different constitution, or, if you like, a special set of rules for operating the Philadelphia Constitution which most of us have taken to heart, adopted in our hearts as our very own, and which in fact govern our political life almost as completely as if they *were* in fact our Constitution. The idea that we have three separate and coordinate branches comes to us not from the Constitution, which is a legislative supremacy constitution, but from *The Federalist,* which lays down for us a constitutional morality, a political ethos that is as natural to us as the air we breathe. Congress does not forget that it possesses the ultimate weapons; it simply believes, as *The Federalist* teaches it to believe, that it *ought* not to use them—that it ought, as the supreme branch, to treat the other two branches *as* equal and co-ordinate. And similarly, *The Federalist* teaches the other two branches that *they* must act merely as equal and co-ordinate branches and not throw *their* weight around. The three branches, *The Federalist* instructs us, are to move together—a requirement which, let us notice, may require any one of the three to spin its wheels for a while until the others are ready to move in the direction in which it wants to go. To put this otherwise: *The Federalist* instructs us, as a matter not of constitutional law but of constitutional morality, that none of the three branches shall force a showdown with the other branches. Nor is there anything more remarkable in our history as a nation than this: There never has been a showdown, and this despite the fact that the Philadelphia Constitution from beginning to end simply invites a showdown. The mystery, we say, disappears when we approach it as a problem not of constitutional law—as we are much in the habit of doing today—but as a matter of constitutional morality that we in America not only believe in, cherish in our hearts as something we ought to obey, but actually practice. We have a duty, if we are Supreme Court justices, not to force a showdown with Congress—not so much because we will lose, though we will, but because the political system held up to us by *The Federalist* obviously cannot survive such showdowns. We have a duty, if we are Congressmen, not to force a showdown with the Supreme Court—not because we have any doubts about whether we will win, but because the American political system, as we have interpreted it for ourselves, requires that there shall be no such confrontations.

What we have said to this point reveals, in its own way, the extent of our derailment. The "new" tradition, and let us call it that for now, seems to overlook or ignore the central teachings of *The Federalist,* teachings which do render our constitutional machinery workable within the context of our traditional symbols. The "new" morality, as we have already indicated, is a long way from accepting any such notions about legislative supremacy, forebearance, or deliberate sense of the community. Instead, its proponents look to institutions other than the Congress for the advancement and even explication of the American tradition. There is, and we believe we do them no injustice in so saying, a certain impatience with those institutions and processes designed, so it would seem, to collect the sense of the community and operate within the confines of the consensual politics of which we have spoken. Indeed, from *their point of view* we could hardly expect anything but impatience. The Declaration of Independence, *as they read it* (quite improperly and arbitrarily in our view) , does hold up certain goals, the foremost of which over the years has become *equality* in the sense of making all humans equal through positive governmental action. But the system, operating under the traditional symbols, has failed to produce the kind and degree of equality which the proponents of the new tradition envision. The Bill of Rights, *as they read it and interpret it,* also holds out certain ends, the foremost of which has again, over the years, become that of the "open" society. Yet, as if to say "no deal," the American people, acting principally through Congress, have shown great reluctance to move in this direction.

There is, to put the matter somewhat differently, an impatience among some with our consensual system. The Declaration of Independence and the Bill of Rights—when they are read out of the context of the traditional symbols—can be interpreted to provide us with a new tradition which presumes to know the answers to those questions which have plagued every society of which we have any recorded history. This tradition so much as tells us, as a people, what our commitments, goals, and mission in history are. Thus, the impatience with that tradition—we believe our true tradition—embodying the symbols of self-government through deliberative processes such as that spelled out in *The Federalist*. So, too, we find that the new tradition provides us with the rationale (and a very elaborate rationale it is) for upholding the most extravagant claims of those institutions, the Presidency, and more notably the Supreme Court, which, so the new tradition tells us, not only have the authority but also the duty to advance our presumed commitments. So it is that our heroes today, at least within intellectual circles where the new tradition predominates, are the Warrens, Blacks, Douglases, along with the Wilsons, Roosevelts I and II, and Lincolns.

We have been speaking to this point, we hasten to emphasize, only about the superficial manifestations of our derailment.[2] The causes of the derailment are far deeper and more complicated than we have suggested. Voegelin teaches us that sets of basic symbols, throughout the West, tend to be variants of the myth of Moses, of the symbols of Egypt: Desert, Covenant, and Promised Land. They are all subject to one variant or another of the kinds of derailments that happened to the people of Israel as chronicled by the Old Testament. The derailments run, as Voegelin tells us, pretty much to type, and assume forms that are not too difficult to identify. One derailment, for example, takes the form of forgetting that the truh

2 We speak at a level, we can go so far as to say, at which most contemporary discourse on these problems takes place. For a further exploration of these and similar matters, see George W. Carey, "Dialogue: Sophistic or Academic," *Phalanx* (Winter, 1968).

of the soul and the truth of society are transcendent truths, and that the function of the basic symbols is to express the relations between political society and God. The basic symbols may be so manipulated as to leave God out altogether, to cut man off from anything and everything higher than himself in the constitution of being, to set man up as God, to understand man as possessing final truth, instead of merely groping for it across the gulf of transcendence. This represents a very fundamental derailment and the most dangerous one. We should hardly be surprised when we find people who experience this form of derailment being terribly sure that they are right and everybody else not only wrong, but wrong because of their wickedness and perversity. People who have suffered such a derailment, we understand at once, are not likely to enjoy waiting for a deliberate sense of the community, and are not likely to content themselves with any process of persuasion and conviction. They *know* they are *right*.

Another typical derailment takes the form of seizing on a single basic symbol that belongs to and was originally set forth in the context of a cluster of symbols and exaggerating it at the expense of the remainder—for example, majority rule at the expense of the deliberate sense of the community; or equality, originally understood as an equal capacity on the part of all men to give or withhold their consent, may be seized upon and exaggerated until it becomes a demand that all men be made equal in every respect, and at whatever cost to life, liberty, and pursuit of happiness on the part of others.

Yet another derailment, a very common one indeed, takes the form of deciding that the Promised Land, the ideal society of saints, can be built in this world, and need not be postponed until the world to come. Marxism is the very embodiment of a derailment of this nature. and we cannot help but notice that the kind of people who go in for it aren't very much concerned with the deliberate sense of any community. Give them, even a small minority of them, the power, and they will proceed to work their way with nary a thought about how others may feel.

And still another derailment takes the form of a belief that you can remake human nature, that you can create, through manipulation of your neighbors, a new and superior breed of men, made in *your* image just as the God of the original symbols made Adam in His image.[3]

These represent the typical derailments, and those who are victimized by them are pretty certain to become fanatics of a sort. They will, each in his own way, demonstrate by their behavior a contempt for the rules laid down in *The Federalist* for the operation of the Philadelphia Constitution. They are the very ones most likely to kick over the traces of the American political system, to manipulate our tradition to suit their fancy, and to insist that such and such be done no matter what the conseqences. So we may safely say: Whenever there is any considerable number of them amongst us, the American political system is on the threshold of a crisis, in danger, that is, of breaking down.

Bearing this in mind, let us return to the American tradition. We have seen the purposes of the American civil body politic presented in embryonic form in the Mayflower Compact, wherein the signers interpret themselves and understand themselves as committed to the glorification of God and the advancement of the faith. Over and against these purposes we also see a solemn commitment to enact just and equal laws, that is, *laws thought to be* (we must never forget this) just and equal, or, more precisely, thought to be *meet and convenient* for the general good.

In Virginia, a century and a half later, some things have

---

3 Publius, let us duly note, is in no way guilty (whatever else his critics may say about him) of contributing to or nourishing any of the forms of derailment.

changed, while others seem to remain the same. The Virginians, though still determined to glorify God and advance the faith, have driven a wedge between government, the political order, and society: If God is to be glorified and the faith advanced, that is to be the business of the American society, operating through the processes of persuasion and conviction. What the American government is to do, above all, is to promote the general good, now understood to be first, a matter of serving the ends of justice, temperance, frugality, virtue, etc.; and second, a matter of serving these ends by turning the job of day-to-day government over to the representative assembly which has supreme power, but power that it is to exercise under God and always with the understanding that the legislative assembly is, according to its best lights, to do justice, to give the individuals out among the people those individual rights that, from the standpoint of justice, they ought to have. And yes, a danger does present itself: The legislative assembly may act too hastily, may not take into account all the considerations that it ought to take into account. What is more, a mere majority of the legislative assembly may act, may even act in good conscience as regards justice, *without* taking into account all that it ought to take into account. The majority may be so sure it is right about what is just that it feels no need to deliberate or even to talk things over. Even the Philadelphia Constitution gives us no solution to that problem for it, too, leaves the majorities of the legislative assembly free to throw their weight around—to refuse to deliberate, to reach for its weapons when someone, anyone, attempts to thwart them. Here, as we have already seen, is where the political morality of the "Federalist Papers" comes in: It teaches us a morality of conciliation, moderation, and, above all, deliberation. The branches of our government, especially Congress, should, according to *The Federalist* morality, avoid a showdown which would be destructive to the very structure created by the Philadelphia Constitution. Congress *should* treat the other two branches as equal and co-ordinate, if for no other reason than to guarantee that the viewpoints, opinions, and considerations of these branches will be given their due weight. Congress *must* and *should*, week after week, month after month, and even, in some cases, year after year, keep on deliberating until, to all intents and purposes, all agree. That is what the teachings and morality of the "Federalist Papers" require the majority of Congress to do; just as Congress must not act until it can carry with it the President and the Supreme Court, so the majority of Congress must not act until it can carry with it the minority—at least to the extent that it will not leave any minority determined (as otherwise it might be) to sabotage the new legislative act. And we need, in this connection, to remember: We have in America no experience, any more than that of the signers of the Mayflower Compact, of a *deliberation* that leaves us with a dissident minority, a minority that proclaims its intention to disobey the law that Congress enacts. One might well say that in America, in accordance with the constitutional morality set down by *The Federalist,* "We the People" act in a very special manner to produce unanimity, obeying the basic rule: The majority must carry the minority along with it, because all men are equal, as they were in the saloon of the Mayflower, in their capacity to give or withhold their consent.

What we come to is this: The basic American symbols, as we have noticed when we spoke about the Mayflower compact, breathe the spirit of moderation, which, we have noticed, has become quite explicit by the time we get to the Virginia Declaration of Rights. They treat the problem of what we are to do, where we the people are going with our government, as a problem that we must think about, and think *together* about. As the "Federalist Papers" put it, the system based on these symbols calls for action by the *deliberate sense of the commu-*

nity, not action by mere majority vote. To be sure, the majority, according to *The Federalist,* has its role in the system; but that role, as we begin to understand, is that of midwifing and then declaring and announcing to the world the sense, the opinion, that the whole community has arrived at through the process of deliberation—which, as we now see, requires that "We the People" proceed with little catsteps.[4] When, therefore, back in Massachusetts, we found them saying that it is the business of government to carry out the truth of the gospel, and the discipline of the churches (obligations which we find in many of our early documents), we did not hesitate to describe this as ominous, for, as we well know, people feel very strongly about the truth of the gospel and the discipline of the churches. Thus we sighed the sigh of relief when we got to Virginia and found the Americans ready to separate the political order from the religious order. And we sighed the same sigh when we found that the Philadelphia Constitution also drives a wedge between politics and religion. The system begins with the spirit of moderation in the political order, and, after Massachusetts, works its way back to the spirit of moderation and to the rules laid down in *The Federalist.*

The system begins, one might say, by an act of consensus in the saloon of the Mayflower, and ends up with acts of consensus, acts of the deliberate sense of the community, as its central political rite, to be reenacted at Philadelphia and, we can now add, in each and every session of Congress. One of the virtues of a virtuous people, we begin to see, one of the virtues that, as individuals, they must cultivate, is that of not expecting the political order, the government, to reflect and act upon the beliefs that they, as individuals, hold most strongly. They are free, as individuals, free over in the social order, to plead the case for the beliefs that they hold most strongly. Unless they

4 See Kendall and Carey, "The Intensity Problem and Democratic Theory," *American Political Science Review* (March, 1968).

make solemn bores of themselves, we the people will listen to them. They can try through the processes of persuasion to build a consensus around their strongly held beliefs, but one virtue they must cultivate is that of not being in too much of a hurry, and another is that of not expecting other people, their neighbors, to give up overnight their *own* strongly held beliefs.

We can put this in another way. The system requires of us that we learn the virtue of patience, along with the virtue of accepting, and accepting with good grace, political defeat. And we should begin to understand why the system has room for institutions that seem to force us into such a morality, even though by all outward evidences they also seem to thwart the will of mere majorities within our society. But all of this, we hasten to add, is foreign to those who presume to know the truths of our tradition, weaned as they are on that literature which tells them that our basic symbols are contained in the Declaration of Independence and the Bill of Rights.

To return to the basic framework which Voegelin provides us. The basic myth, in terms of which the American people have traditionally represented themselves and created their own world of meaning, runs something as follows (that it happens to be historically true, as we believe, is the least important thing about it) : The American people lived originally in that wicked and darkest of most oppressive places Europe (=Egypt). Yes, some might well laugh at this equation, but such a teaching, albeit in different terms, was commonplace and well understood and accepted up to a relatively recent time. The wickedness of Europe is a fundamental presupposition of our central myth: The American people "lived" in Europe, where they suffered tyranny and oppression, where, above all, they were not permitted to worship God according to the dictates of their own consciences. They dream a dream— of a promised land, off there in the Canaan (= America) , that lies beyond the desert (=Atlantic Ocean) where they *will* be able to worship God according to the dictates of their own consciences. They decide, rather remarkably but quite in keeping with the myth which keeps on warning that they are a rather special lot, to be their own Moses and lead *themselves* out of Egypt. They pause for a moment in Holland, which is, of course, the wrong direction, then sail across the desert to the border of the Promised Land—and there naturally enough re-enact (in the form of a covenant with one another) the very covenant of the people of Israel at Mount Sinai, giving it the name of the Mayflower Compact and adopting it as one of their highest symbols. Once ashore, they discover, rather to their surprise, two things: First, they are not only free to worship God as they like—free because there is no one to tell them, besides themselves, how to govern and impose rules upon them; and second, they soon learn, in the absence of some authority to rule them, to govern themselves. This for them was a real problem, for the simple reason that it has been a long time since Greece and Rome, and understandably enough, they have only the haziest memory about that which we call self-government. Speedily, in any case, they discover self-government, thè problem of how a people goes about governing itself, as their peculiar problem, which they conceive as a matter of making and remaking the Mayflower Compact, of experimenting with this or that variant of the symbolization of the Mayflower Compact.

But for all of this let us point out the following: They do not kid themselves that the Promised Land, the real and genuine Promised Land, can be built in this world. They content themselves with the more modest idea of building a promised land that will be merely decent and orderly—the very opposite, of course, of that indecent and disorderly Europe from which they emerged. They do not kid themselves either that they can remake human nature: Men, they know, are great sinners, potentially prideful, lustful, deceiving even, though also, happily, capable of a certain amount of virtue which ought to be cultivated and developed. Finally, because of their good sense, they do not regard the world, the world out there beyond the two oceans, as their particular oyster; at their most typical, happily or unhappily, their thought about the big wide world is that it can go to hell at sunset. They have no desire or dream to build an empire that will include all of mankind, though all of mankind does, in due course, come to figure in their thinking about themselves. They come finally to the idea, stated at the beginning of the "Federalist Papers," that they are the suffering servants of mankind (never, however, suffering very badly, never suffering in a way that prevents a little groaning under their burden of turkey and ham on Thanksgiving Day), called upon to set an example to mankind by discovering the answer to the question: How is the people to govern itself without being tyrannical? If we may put it so, the answer to this question is found in two pieces of our sacred scripture (The Constitution and *The Federalist*) which add up to the following rules: Thou shalt govern thyselves under God, through the deliberate sense of the community, of the generality of men amongst thee; thou shalt respect certain procedures necessary for that purpose; thou shalt avoid fanaticism; thou shalt preserve thy sense of humor, remembering that pride goeth before a fall; thou shalt try, above all, to be a virtuous people, made up of virtuous individuals, because only a virtuous people can do justice, remain untyrannical, as it governs itself through deliberation about the general good.

Now, in these very same terms, we can describe the typical derailments that have plagued the American tradition. One derailment runs as follows: God does not exist, but the American people are still the chosen people who must, because God does not exist, build the Promised Land on earth—on earth, of course, because earth is the only place where building is

possible. According to this myth, our national genius expresses itself, not so much in the Constitution and *The Federalist*,
but in an apostolic succession of great leaders: George Washington, Thomas Jefferson, Abraham Lincoln, Roosevelts I and
II, and John Kennedy, each of whom sees more deeply than
the preceding leader into the specifically American problem,
which is posed by the "all men are created equal" clause of
the Declaration of Independence. America will build a New
Jerusalem which will be a commonwealth of free and equal
men. If all of this requires remaking human nature, making
the unequal to be equal—well, no job is too big for the self-
chosen people if it knows its destiny and is determined to
achieve it.

Still another, and more important derailment, holds that
the Moses of the American people is Jehovah himself, who led
them out of the hellhole, Egypt, in order to build, right here
on Earth, the New Jerusalem. The Americans are God's people, America is God's Own Country. In other words, God has
appointed America, not as the suffering servant of mankind,
but as the arbiter of mankind, the supreme judge of all people, with a special insight into Divine Providence that no other people can match. God led the American people out of
Egypt, and when He sees that Egypt won't let it go at that,
He takes over and begins to run America as His Own private
enterprise. He raised up a man, George Washington, a veri-
table paragon of all the virtues, to expel the pursuing Egyptians (who in their wickedness will not obey the command:
Let my people go) from the Promised Land. In due course,
the happy moment comes: The Egyptians have been forced
back into Egypt, which since Egypt is Hell, is where the Eur-
opeans belong, and we, God's own people, can get down to
our proper business, which is building the New Jerusalem and
spreading it over the face of the entire earth. That, of course,
since in the New Jerusalem, the lion will lie down beside the

lamb, involves remaking human nature. But in this account of our tradition this presents no problem: God made human nature to begin with, and we, as God's chosen people, will remake it.

The false myths produce the fanatics amongst us. They are misrepresentations and distortions of the American political tradition and its basic symbols which are, let us remind you, the representative assembly *deliberating* under God; the virtuous people, virtuous because deeply religious and thus committed to the *process* of searching for the transcendent Truth. And these are, we believe, symbols we can be proud of without going before a fall.

Appendix I

We are far from believing that the equality clause of the Declaration is meaningless. What does it mean? Our best guess is that the clause simply asserts the proposition that all peoples who identify themselves as one—that is, those who identify themselves as a society, nation, or state for action in history—are equal to others who have likewise identified themselves. This interpretation seems quite plausible in light of the first paragraph of the Declaration and the passages which immediately follow the equality clause.

We can put our point still another way. The Declaration asserts that Americans are equal to, say, the British and French. If the British and French can claim equality among the sovereign states of the world, so, too, can Americans. This interpretation takes on added force in light of the major purpose of the Declaration. Specifically, the drafters of the Declaration are maintaining that the Americans are equal to the British and are, therefore, as free as the British to establish a form of government which "shall seem most likely to effect their [American] safety and happiness." We think it important to note that equality is not listed among those ends to be secured by government. Equality, in the sense we have just described, is a value employed to justify the separation.

That Lincoln held a markedly different conception of the equality clause is beyond dispute. Although Lincoln did have some very curious notions concerning the meaning of equality (and this even his worshippers cannot deny), he did "internalize" the notion of equality. This is to say that he considered equality a value or goal to be promoted by those who have identified themselves as one. So much seems clear from the Gettysburg Address. Lincoln, in effect, is telling us that we have a commitment as a fully sovereign state to promote equality. If there be any doubts on this score, the Lincoln-Douglas debates, Lincoln's speech at Springfield, Illinois (June 26, 1857), and, among other items, his Message to Congress in Special Session (July 4, 1861) ought to dispel them.

Now, Lincoln's "internalization" of the concept of equality has had, in our judgment, an enormous impact on American scholarship and thinking. Few would deny that many professional students of American government and theory are preoccupied with the question of what equality means within our society given the Lincolnian view of the Declaration. While we believe this to be an intriguing enterprise, we also believe it to be a futile one, given the ground rules provided by Lincoln. From our vantage point, what seems more important is that Lincoln's interpretation has gained such wide and uncritical acceptance among contemporary scholars.

Appendix II

Reproduced here are certain documents or portions thereof that have been cited in the book. The Declaration of Independence, the Constitution, and Lincoln's Gettysburg Address have been omitted because these documents are readily accessible to students.

(A) *The Mayflower Compact.* Original spelling. Source: Benjamin Perley Poore (ed.), *The Federal and State Constitutions, Colonial Charters and other Organic Laws of the United States* (Washington, D.C., Government Printing Office, 1877). Complete text.

AGREEMENT BETWEEN THE SETTLERS
AT NEW PLYMOUTH.

IN THE NAME OF GOD, AMEN. We, whose names are underwritten, the Loyal Subjects of our dread Sovereign Lord King *James,* by the Grace of God, of *Great Britain, France,* and *Ireland,* King, *Defender of the Faith,* &c. Having undertaken for the Glory of God, and Advancement of the Christian Faith, and the Honour of our King and Country, a Voyage to plant the first Colony in the northern Parts of *Virginia*; Do by these Presents, solemnly and mutually, in the Presence of God and one another, covenant and combine ourselves together into a civil Body Politick, for our better Ordering and Preservation, and Furtherance of the Ends aforesaid: And by Virtue hereof do enact, constitute, and frame, such just and equal Laws, Ordinances, Acts, Constitutions, and Officers, from time to time, as shall be thought most meet and convenient for the general Good of the

Colony; unto which we promise all due Submission and Obedience. IN WITNESS whereof we have hereunto subscribed our names at *Cape-Cod* the eleventh of *November,* in the Reign of our Sovereign Lord King *James,* of *England, France,* and *Ireland,* the eighteenth, and of *Scotland,* the fifty-fourth, *Anno Domini,* 1620.

[Signed by 41 individuals]

(B) *The Fundamental Orders of Connecticut.* Original spelling. Source: Benjamin Perley Poore, *op. cit.* Only the first paragraph of this document is reproduced here. The remainder of the document deals almost exclusively with the organization and procedures of government as set forth in the text.

FUNDAMENTAL ORDERS OF CONNECTICUT–1638-'39.

FORASMUCH as it hath pleased the Allmighty God by the wise disposition of his diuyne pᵉuidence so to Order and dispose of things that we the Inhabitants and Residents of Windsor, Harteford and Wethersfield are now cohabiting and dwelling in and vppon the River of Conectecotte and the Lands thereunto adioyneing; And well knowing where a people are gathered together the word of God requires that to mayntayne the peace and vnion of such a people there should be an orderly and decent Gouerment established according to God, to order and dispose of the affayres of the people at all seasons as occation shall require; doe therefore assotiate and conioyne our selues to be as one Publike State or Comonwelth; and doe, for our selues and our Successors and such as shall be adioyned to vs att any tyme hereafter, enter into Combination and Confederation togather, to mayntayne and pᵉsearue the liberty and purity of the gospell of our Lord Jesus wᶜʰ we now pᵉfesse, as also the disciplyne of the Churches, wᶜʰ according to the truth of the said gospell is now practised amongst vs; As also in oᵉ Ciuell Affaires to be guided and gouerned according to such Lawes, Rules, Orders and decrees as shall be made, ordered & decreed, as followeth:—

(C) *The Massachusetts Body of Liberties* (1641). Original spelling. Source: *Colonial Laws of Massachusetts,* compiled by Order of the City Council of Boston under the direction of Mr. S. Whitmore, 1889. Text partial.

A COPPIE OF THE LIBERTIES OF THE
MASSACHUSETS COLONIE IN NEW ENGLAND.

The free fuition of such liberties Immunities and priveledges as humanitie, Civilitie, and Christianitie call for as due to every man in his place and proportion without impeachment and Infringement hath ever bene and ever will be the tranquillitie and Stabilitie of Churches and Commonwealths. And the deniall or deprivall thereof, the disturbance if not the ruine of both.

We hould it therefore our dutie and safetie whilst we are about the further establishing of this Government to collect and expresse all such freedomes as for present we foresee may concerne us, and our posteritie after us, And to ratify them with our sollemne consent. We doe therefore this day religiously and unanimously decree and confirme these following Rites, liberties and priveledges concerneing our Churches, and Civil State to be respectively impartialie and inviolably enjoyed and observed throughout our Jurisdiction for ever.

No mans life shall be taken away, no mans honour or good name shall be stayned, no mans person shall be arested, restrayned, banished, dismembred, nor any wayes punished, no man shall be deprived of his wife or children, no mans goods or estaite shall be taken away from him, nor any way indammaged under coulor of law or Countenance of Authoritie, unlesse it be by vertue or equitie of some expresse law of the Country waranting the same, established by a generall Court and sufficiently published, or in case of the defect of a law in any parteculer case by the word of god. And in Capitall cases, or in cases concerning dismembring or banishment, according to that word to be judged by the Generall Court.

Liberties of Forreiners and Strangers.

If any people of other Nations professing the true Christian Religion shall flee to us from the Tiranny or oppression of their persecutors, or from famyne, warres, or the like necessary and compulsarie cause, They shall be entertayned and succoured amongst us, according to that power and prudence god shall give us.

94. CAPITALL LAWS.

1.

If any man after legall conviction shall have or worship any other god, but the lord god, he shall be put to death.

2.

If any man or woeman be a witch, (that is hath or consulteth with a familiar spirit,) They shall be put to death.

3.

If any man shall Blaspheme the name of god, the father, Sonne or Holie ghost, with direct, expresse, presumptuous or high handed blasphemie, or shall curse god in the like manner, he shall be put to death.

4.

If any person committ any wilfull murther, which is manslaughter, committed upon premeditated mallice, hatred or Crueltie, not in a mans necessarie and just defence, nor by meere casualtie against his will, he shall be put to death.

5.

If any person slayeth an other suddaienly in his anger or Crueltie of passion, he shall be put to death.

6.

If any person shall slay an other through guile, either by poysoning or other such divelish practice, he shall be put to death.

7.

If any man or woeman shall lye with any beaste or bruite creature by Carnall Copulation, They shall surely be put to death. And the beast shall be slaine and buried and not eaten.

8.

If any man lyeth with mankinde as he lyeth with a woeman, both of them have committed abhomination, they both shall surely be put to death.

9.

If any person committeth Adultery with a maried or espoused wife, the Adulterer and Adulteresse shall surely be put to death.

10.

If any man stealeth a man or mankinde, he shall surely be put to death.

11.

If any man rise up by false witnes, wittingly and of purpose to take away any mans life, he shall be put to death.

12.

If any man shall conspire and attempt any invasion, insurrection, or publique rebellion against our commonwealth, or shall indeavour to surprize any Towne or Townes, fort or forts therein, or shall treacherously and perfediouslie attempt the alteration and subversion of our frame of politie or Government fundamentallie, he shall be put to death.

Lastly because our dutie and desire is to do nothing suddainlie which fundamentally concerne us, we decree that these rites and liberties, shall be Audably read and deliberately weighed at every Generall

Court that shall be held, within three yeares next insueing, And such of them as shall not be altered or repealed they shall stand so ratified, That no man shall infringe them without due punishment.

And if any Generall Court within these next thre yeares shall faile or forget to reade and consider them as abovesaid. The Governor and Deputy Governor for the time being, and every Assistant present at such Courts shall forfeite 20sh. a man, and everie Deputie 10sh. a man for each neglect, which shall be paid out of their proper estate, and not by the Country or the Townes which choose them, and whensoever there shall arise any question in any Court amonge the Assistants and Associates thereof about the explanation of these Rites and liberties, The Generall Court onely shall have power to interprett them.

(D) *The Virginia Bill of Rights.* Original spelling. Source: Poore, *op. cit.* Complete text.

VIRGINIA BILL OF RIGHTS—1776.

A declaration of rights made by the representatives of the good people of Virginia, assembled in full and free convention; which rights do pertain to them and their posterity, as the basis and foundation of government.

SECTION 1. That all men are by nature equally free and independent, and have certain inherent rights, of which, when they enter into a state of society, they cannot, by any compact, deprive or divest their posterity; namely, the enjoyment of life and liberty, with the means of acquiring and possessing property, and pursuing and obtaining happiness and safety.

SEC. 2. That all power is vested in, and consequently derived from, the people; that magistrates are their trustees and servants, and at all times amenable to them.

SEC. 3. That government is, or ought to be, instituted for the common benefit, protection, and security of the people, nation, or community; of all the various modes and forms of government, that is best which is capable of producing the greatest degree of happiness and safety, and is most effectually secured against the danger of maladministration; and that, when any government shall be found inadequate or contrary to these purposes, a majority of the community hath an indubitable, inalienable, and indefeasible right to reform, alter, or abolish it, in such manner as shall be judged most conducive to the public weal.

SEC. 4. That no man, or set of men, are entitled to exclusive or separate emoluments or privileges from the community, but in consideration of public services; which, not being descendible, neither ought the offices of magistrate, legislator, or judge to be hereditary.

SEC. 5. That the legislative and executive powers of the State should be separate and distinct from the judiciary; and that the members of the two first may be restrained from oppression, by feeling and participating the burdens of the people, they should, at fixed periods, be reduced to a private station, return into that body from which they were originally taken, and the vacancies be supplied by frequent, certain, and regular elections, in which all, or any part of the former members, to be again eligible, or ineligible, as the laws shall direct.

SEC. 6. That elections of members to serve as representatives of the people, in assembly, ought to be free; and that all men, having sufficient evidence of permanent common interest with, and attachment to, the community, have the right of suffrage, and cannot be taxed or deprived of their property for public uses, without their own consent, or that of their representatives so elected, nor bound by any law to which they have not, in like manner, assented, for the public good.

SEC. 7. That all power of suspending laws, or the execution of laws, by any authority, without consent of the representatives of the people, is injurious to their rights, and ought not to be exercised.

SEC. 8. That in all capital or criminal prosecutions a man hath a right to demand the cause and nature of his accusation, to be confronted with the accusers and witnesses, to call for evidence in his favor, and to a speedy trial by an impartial jury of twelve men of his vicinage, without whose unanimous consent he cannot be found guilty; nor can he be compelled to give evidence against himself; that no man be deprived of his liberty, except by the law of the land or the judgment of his peers.

SEC. 9. That excessive bail ought not to be required, nor excessive fines imposed, nor cruel and unusual punishments inflicted.

SEC. 10. That general warrants, whereby an officer or messenger may be commanded to search suspected places without evidence of a fact committed, or to seize any person or persons not named, or whose offence is not particularly described and supported by evidence, are grievous and oppressive, and ought not to be granted.

Sec. 11. That in controversies respecting property, and in suits between man and man, the ancient trial by jury is preferable to any other, and ought to be held sacred.

Sec. 12. That the freedom of the press is one of the great bulwarks of liberty, and can never be restrained but by despotic governments.

Sec. 13. That a well-regulated militia, composed of the body of the people, trained to arms, is the proper, natural, and safe defence of a free State; that standing armies, in time of peace, should be avoided, as dangerous to liberty; and that in all cases the military should be under strict subordination to, and governed by, the civil power.

Sec. 14. That the people have a right to uniform government; and, therefore, that no government separate from, or independent of the government of Virginia, ought to be erected or established within the limits thereof.

Sec. 15. That no free government, or the blessings of liberty, can be preserved to any people, but by a firm adherence to justice, moderation, temperance, frugality, and virtue, and by frequent recurrence to fundamental principles.

Sec. 16. That religion, or the duty which we owe to our Creator, and the manner of discharging it, can be directed only by reason and conviction, not by force or violence; and therefore all men are equally entitled to the free exercise of religion, according to the dictates of conscience; and that it is the mutual duty of all to practise Christian forbearance, love, and charity towards each other.

Index

165